CM09287756

STÉPHANE MALLARMÉ

Selected Poems

STÉPHANE MALLARMÉ
From a lithograph by Whistler

STÉPHANE MALLARMÉ

SELECTED

POEMS

Translated by
C. F. MacINTYRE

UNIVERSITY OF CALIFORNIA PRESS
Berkeley, Los Angeles, London

University of California Press
Berkeley and Los Angeles, California
University of California Press, Ltd.
London, England

© *1957 by*
The Regents of the University of California
ISBN: 0-520-00801-4
Library of Congress Catalogue Card No. 57-10505

Designed by Rita Carroll
Printed in the United States of America

DEDICATION

Dear Harold:

This is one item in my book I sternly forbid you to touch. It is practically the only page of those your press has published for me that is all mine own. During the past—almost a score of years—you have repeatedly cast me into utter despair when you astutely discovered a boner, some difficulty I'd funked, thinking how cleverly it was concealed.

You have taken hours, months, years from my life and hair from my worried poll, robbed me of sleep and content, through beautiful white nights when "the lamp burned low" and you bedeviled me toward your vision of the ultimate almost perfection. That I could never quite satisfy, but how I tried! After hours of work in the library when you ran some Reynardly tricky reference to his "earth," you have taken my name in vain when you let it stand as mine after I had gratefully made acknowledgment. Of all your sins that is the most egregious and culpable. Really, the truth has not been in you. I herewith restore credit to whom it is due.

With your delicate "Well, if you could . . ." you have given me insomnia, attacks of spleen, and desperation, with a pat on the head when sometimes I was finally able to do what you wanted. A man of parts, you have, with Bellerophonic buttocks, stoutly bestridden my flighty Pegasus as you guided his frail flight toward

Parnassus. Of the dozen editors with whom I have fought successively my Waterloos, you have been the most indefatigable, painstaking, accurate, and demandingly helpful; hence, it is with high delight that I dedicate this, the sixth of our collaborations, justly and affectionately, to you. Stet.

C.F.M.

PREFACE

August the twenty-fifth, Day of the Liberation of
Paris! A grand tricolor is flapping in the Arc de Tri-
omphe, above the Tomb of the Unknown Soldier. The
Champs Elysées, gay with summer dresses, bright para-
sols, soldiers in splendid uniforms with red plumes,
sidewalk cafés where the tables are brilliant with glasses
of pink grenadine, green mint, brown apéritifs, red
wines or brown beer . . . glittering cars creep in the
holiday traffic, neatly trimmed poodles strain at leashes,
sleek girls on display glide proudly past, eyeing their
reflections in the shop windows, on which elderly ladies
from the Middle West of the United States are rub-
bing their noses in search of bargains; rejuvenated
businessmen are looking for naughty postcards to shock
the boys back home; great barelegged Germans with
knapsacks stride muscularly up the slight grade—it
must be with a certain chagrin that they remember the
late occupation; a score of girls from a boarding school
march primly along in blue uniforms, shepherded by
two grim-faced teachers. A charming mannequin, or is
she a high-powered tart on a cruise? The eternal vendor
of rainbow balloons, a little boy who wants to make
pipi, some old women shuffling in felt-soled slippers,
clutching string bags, a drunk panhandling, a cripple
with a tray of plastic toys. And from the sycamore
trees, bordering the avenue, already drift brown-edged

warnings that this paradisal weather is the last period of grace.

Day of the Liberation! I wish I could say as much for me! But I have just bought another copy of the *Ouverture ancienne d'Hérodiade* and sit on a *terrasse* to cut the pages. Within five minutes I can sadly summarize again the numberless hours of joy and despair, of rage and rapture, of confidence and frustration that I have spent over Mallarmé's thin volume since 1939 when I thought I'd just translate one of them 'for fun.' Then, like the Lesbia of Catullus—*odi et amo*—but I couldn't give it up. Meanwhile I began and have now published selections from three of his contemporaries: Baudelaire, Verlaine, and Corbière, but Mallarmé has been like the Old Man of the Sea, like the Biblical poor. There's no getting rid of him!

In this *"Ouverture,"* so long stupidly withheld from publication by the poet's son-in-law, a reader finds grounds for all his grievances against the author. A weird and difficult music is being played, almost anonymously, in some musty room in a half-ruined tower: the incantation of an old nurse who utters a delirious gibberish, almost toothless mumblings from the subconscious. The poet's arbitrary suppression of syntax, his violations of grammar, the overuse of the same word or symbol, and his deliberate obfuscating of an otherwise charming scene or speech are all immediately annoying. One begins to suffocate for lack of oxygen, the true poetic afflatus. Why, he asks himself, should

viii

I continue to bother with this willful abracadabra? The answer is: Let him beware, or he will fall under the spell of the little master and be henceforth caught in the springe, as were such illustrious contemporaries as Yeats, Rilke, Heredia, Gide, Valéry, D'Annunzio, Stefan George, Joyce, Verhaeren, Coppée, Villiers, Verlaine, and dozens of lesser talents.

One of the poet's best critics, Albert Thibaudet, has written: ". . . His ideal would be to write the characters (like Chinese ideographs) in juxtaposition, with neither phrase nor grammatical logic; no order of syntax would deform the purity of the words . . . the verb form most employed is the infinitive . . . and often the verb disappears as useless, descriptive and oratorical." In the face of this slight sample of the difficulties listed by an enthusiast, I can say only: Listen again to the Prelude for *L'Après-midi d'un Faune,* for Debussy will long remain one of the best guides into the mysterious realm of Mallarmé, and it is finally as pure music that he is best apprehended and enjoyed. As for understanding—that is another matter. Remy de Gourmont has said it better: "Mallarmé is the best pretext for reveries."

In the struggle between the frozen lack of communication on the printed page and the fascination afforded by an occasional glimpse into something rich and strange, the reader is battered about like a shuttlecock. But just when he is most annoyed, bored with these unsolvable riddles, maybe an indelible phrase will strike him and, like Saul on the road to Damascus, he will be ever afterward a changed man. Even his peers and colleagues, many of whom are mentioned above, who attended reverently the famous Tuesday evenings in the cramped apartment on the rue de Rome, were never able to record the marvelous monologues he uttered, while rolling and smoking innumerable cigarettes. And there were, *hélas,* no tape recorders. But he did say: "La Pénultième . . . est morte," which might have been his own epitaph, for with the death of perhaps his most faithful disciple Valéry, Symbolism, as a literary movement, may be said to have been ended.

The appended bibliography will make apparent how impossible it would have been, in a book of this kind, to have attempted a symposium of the criticisms of the poet's subject matter, form, method, and style. There is no faithful little Geiger counter that has adequately divulged the secret lodes in the few books. Every specialist has his own private patch wherein he believes the secret lies. Most of my slight tailings are implicit in the attempted translations, but I shouldn't even have managed these had I not been 'grubstaked,' so to speak, by the patient help of Mlle Jacqueline de La Harpe, who gave me the first encouragement, and made me aware of the almost feminine intuitive method of approach I have found to be better than any logical attempt to parse and analyze the difficulties. Dozens of others—I hope I've forgotten none, but some asked to remain anonymous—Yvonne Templin, Professors Mathurin Dondo, Francis Carmody, Warren Ramsey, Alvin

Eustis, and any number of casual contacts with French experts and enthusiasts who finally offered maybe a phrase or suggestion (for in Paris every intellectual is very busy grinding his own ax, and no one has time for conferences) have helped me to get this book finished. But, as usual, it has been the patient and always practical readings and notes of the editor which have tugged me through the slough of Despond. And now, as indicated in the dedication, this book becomes his spiritual property in 'perpetuity.'

Paris, 1957   C.F.M.

CONTENTS

Voix étrangère . . .
. . . par nul écho suivie,
L'oiseau qu'on n'ouït jamais
Une autre fois en la vie.

THE POEMS

SALUT

RIEN, cette écume, vierge vers
A ne désigner que la coupe;
Telle loin se noie une troupe
De sirènes mainte à l'envers.

Nous naviguons, ô mes divers
Amis, moi déjà sur la poupe
Vous l'avant fastueux qui coupe
Le flot de foudres et d'hivers;

Une ivresse belle m'engage
Sans craindre même son tangage
De porter debout ce salut

Solitude, récif, étoile
A n'importe ce qui valut
Le blanc souci de notre toile.

SALUT

Nothing, this foam, virgin verse
denoting only the cup;
thus far away drowns a troop
of sirens many reversed.

We sail, O my diverse
friends, I by now on the poop
you the dashing prow that sunders
the surge of winters and thunders;

a lovely glow prevails
in me without fear of the pitch
to offer upright this toast

Solitude, star, rock-coast
to that no matter which
worth the white concern of our sail.

PLACET FUTILE

PRINCESSE! à jalouser le destin d'une Hébé
Qui poind sur cette tasse au baiser de vos lèvres,
J'use mes feux mais n'ai rang discret que d'abbé
Et ne figurerai même nu sur le Sèvres.

Comme je ne suis pas ton bichon embarbé,
Ni la pastille ni du rouge, ni jeux mièvres
Et que sur moi je sais ton regard clos tombé,
Blonde dont les coiffeurs divins sont des orfèvres!

Nommez-nous... toi de qui tant de ris framboisés
Se joignent en troupeau d'agneaux apprivoisés
Chez tous broutant les vœux et bêlant aux délires,

Nommez-nous... pour qu'Amour ailé d'un éventail
M'y peigne flûte aux doigts endormant ce bercail,
Princesse, nommez-nous berger de vos sourires.

PLACET FUTILE

PRINCESS! jealous of the fate of a Hebe
who dawns upon this cup to the kiss of your lips,
I waste my fires but have only slight rank as abbé
and shall not even appear naked on the Sèvres cup.

Since I am not your whiskered poodle, nor
lozenge, rouge, nor an affected pose
and since I know your glance toward me is closed,
blonde for whom goldsmiths are divine coiffeurs!

appoint us . . . you in whose laughter so many wild
berries join a flock of gentle lambs
nibbling at all vows, bleating with delight,

appoint us . . . so that Love wing'd with a fan
paint me there, flute in fingers to lull this fold,
Princess, appoint us shepherd of your smiles.

UNE NÉGRESSE...

UNE négresse par le démon secouée
Veut goûter une enfant triste de fruits nouveaux
Et criminels aussi sous leur robe trouée,
Cette goinfre s'apprête à de rusés travaux:

A son ventre compare heureuses deux tétines
Et, si haut que la main ne le saura
   saisir,
Elle darde le choc obscur de ses bottines
Ainsi que quelque langue inhabile au plaisir.

Contre la nudité peureuse de gazelle
Qui tremble, sur le dos tel un fol éléphant
Renversée elle attend et s'admire avec zèle,
En riant de ses dents naïves à l'enfant;

Et, dans ses jambes où la victime se couche,
Levant une peau noire ouverte sous le crin,
Avance le palais de cette étrange bouche
Pâle et rose comme un coquillage marin.

UNE NÉGRESSE...

A NEGRESS who has been possessed by the devil
wants to taste a young child saddened by these evil
and strange fruits underneath her tattered garments,
a sly trick is got ready by this gourmand:

on her belly she compares two jolly dugs
and, so high that a hand will not know how to seize
  her,
she thrusts the dark shock of her booted legs
even as some tongue unskilled in pleasure.

Near the timid nudity of trembling gazelle,
flat on her back like an elephant gone wild
she waits as she admires herself with zeal,
laughing with her white teeth at the child;

then, between her legs where the victim rests,
in the mane lifting the black open fell,
the palate of this uncouth mouth is thrust
pale and rosy as an ocean shell.

LES FENÊTRES

Las du triste hôpital, et de l'encens fétide
Qui monte en la blancheur banale des rideaux
Vers le grand crucifix ennuyé du mur vide,
Le moribond sournois y redresse un vieux dos,

Se traîne et va, moins pour chauffer sa pourriture
Que pour voir du soleil sur les pierres, coller
Les poils blancs et les os de la maigre figure
Aux fenêtres qu'un beau rayon clair veut hâler,

Et la bouche, fiévreuse et d'azur bleu vorace,
Telle, jeune, elle alla respirer son trésor,
Une peau virginale et de jadis! encrasse
D'un long baiser amer les tièdes carreaux d'or.

Ivre, il vit, oubliant l'horreur des saintes huiles,
Les tisanes, l'horloge et le lit infligé,
La toux; et quand le soir saigne parmi les tuiles,
Son œil, à l'horizon de lumière gorgé,

Voit des galères d'or, belles comme des cygnes,
Sur un fleuve de pourpre et de parfums dormir
En berçant l'éclair fauve et riche de leurs lignes
Dans un grand nonchaloir chargé de souvenir!

Ainsi, pris du dégoût de l'homme à l'âme dure
Vautré dans le bonheur, où ses seuls appétits
Mangent, et qui s'entête à chercher cette ordure
Pour l'offrir à la femme allaitant ses petits,

Je fuis et je m'accroche à toutes les croisées
D'où l'on tourne l'épaule à la vie, et, béni,

8

LES FENÊTRES

TIRED of the dull hospital and fetid smell
rising into the banal white of the curtains
toward the large bored cross of the empty wall,
this dying dissembler, dragging himself, straightens

an aged back and goes, less to warm his rot
than to look at the sunlight on the stones,
to glue his white hair and thin body's bones
to the windows a bright sun-ray tries to bronze,

and the mouth, feverish and greedy for the blue azure,
as once when young it used to inhale its treasure,
a skin virginal and of long-ago! has fouled
with a long bitter kiss the tepid panes of gold.

Drunk, he lives, forgetting the horror of holy oils,
the infusions, the clock, the inflicted bed, the tight
cough; and when evening bleeds along the tiles,
his eyes, on the horizon gorged with light,

see golden galleys, beautiful as swans,
sleeping on a river of crimson and fragrance
cradling their lines of rich and savage bronze
in a deep apathy charged with remembrance!

Thus, seized with disgust for the man of vulgar spirit
wallowing in luck, where his belly's fed,
and who hunts this ordure stubbornly to share it
with the woman who suckles his little brood,

I fly and I clutch tightly to the windows
whence one turns shoulder toward life; in their bright

9

Dans leur verre, lavé d'éternelles rosées,
Que dore le matin chaste de l'Infini

Je me mire et me vois ange! et je meurs, et j'aime
—Que la vitre soit l'art, soit la mysticité—
A renaître, portant mon rêve en diadème,
Au ciel antérieur où fleurit la Beauté!

Mais, hélas! Ici-bas est maître: sa hantise
Vient m'écœurer parfois jusqu'en cet abri sûr,
Et le vomissement impur de la Bêtise
Me force à me boucher le nez devant l'azur.

Est-il moyen, ô Moi qui connais l'amertume,
D'enfoncer le cristal par le monstre insulté
Et de m'enfuir, avec mes deux ailes sans plume
—Au risque de tomber pendant l'éternité?

glass, bless'd, bathed by eternal dews,
gilt by the chaste dawn of the Infinite,

I admire myself, see me as angel! I die, I adore
—may the glass be art, may it be mysticity—
to be reborn, with my dream a crown for me,
in the anterior sky where Beauty flowers!

But, alas, Here-below is master, his intimacy
sickens me sometimes in this certain shelter,
and the dirty vomit of Stupidity
makes me hold my nose before the azure.

Are there ways, O Self who know asperity,
to break the crystal outraged by this monster
and to escape, on these wings without feathers
—at the risk of falling throughout eternity?

ANGOISSE

Je ne viens pas ce soir vaincre ton corps, ô bête
En qui vont les péchés d'un peuple, ni creuser
Dans tes cheveux impurs une triste tempête
Sous l'incurable ennui que verse mon baiser:

Je demande à ton lit le lourd sommeil sans songes
Planant sous les rideaux inconnus du
    remords,
Et que tu peux goûter après tes noirs mensonges
Toi qui sur le néant en sait plus que les morts.

Car le Vice, rongeant ma native noblesse
M'a comme toi marqué de sa stérilité,
Mais tandis que ton sein de pierre est habité

Par un cœur que la dent d'aucun crime ne blesse,
Je fuis, pâle, défait, hanté par mon linceul,
Ayant peur de mourir lorsque je couche seul.

ANGOISSE

I DO not come tonight to conquer your flesh,
O beast with the sins of the race, nor in your impure
hair to stir up a melancholy tempest
by the fatal ennui that my kisses pour:

I ask but to sleep soundly in your bed
where no dreams lurk under curtains unknown to
    regret,
sleep you can savor past your black deceits,
you who know more of Nothing than the dead:

for Vice, corroding my nobility
inborn, brands both with its sterility,
but while there lives within your breast of stone

a heart no tooth of any crime can prod,
wasted and pale and haunted by my shroud,
I flee, afraid to die if I sleep alone.

TRISTESSE D'ÉTÉ

LE SOLEIL, sur le sable, ô lutteuse endormie,
En l'or de tes cheveux chauffe un bain langoureux
Et, consumant l'encens sur ta joue ennemie,
Il mêle avec les pleurs un breuvage amoureux.

De ce blanc flamboiement l'immuable accalmie
T'a fait dire, attristée, ô mes baisers peureux,
"Nous ne serons jamais une seule momie
Sous l'antique désert et les palmiers heureux!"

Mais ta chevelure est une rivière tiède,
Où noyer sans frissons l'âme qui nous obsède
Et trouver ce Néant que tu ne connais pas!

Je goûterai le fard pleuré par tes paupières,
Pour voir s'il sait donner au cœur que tu frappas
L'insensibilité de l'azur et des pierres.

TRISTESSE D'ÉTÉ

THE sunlight on the sand, O wrestler asleep,
is heating a languorous bath in your golden hair
and, burning the incense on your enemy cheek,
it mingles an amorous potion with the tears.

Of this white blazing the immutable calm
(O my timid kisses!) has made you sadly wonder:
"Will we ever be one mummy under
the ancient desert and the happy palms?"

But your thick tresses are a tepid river
to drown the soul that haunts us, without shudders,
to find this Nothingness to you unknown!

I'll taste the rouge by your eyes overwept,
to see if it can give the heart you've whipped
the indifference of azure and of stones.

AUMÔNE

PRENDS ce sac, Mendiant! tu ne le cajolas
Sénile nourrisson d'une tétine avare
Afin de pièce à pièce en égoutter ton glas.

Tire du métal cher quelque péché bizarre
Et vaste comme nous, les poings pleins, le baisons.
Souffles-y qu'il se torde! une ardente fanfare.

Eglise avec l'encens que toutes ces maisons
Sur les murs quand berceur d'une bleue éclaircie
Le tabac sans parler roule les oraisons,

Et l'opium puissant brise la pharmacie!
Robes et peau, veux-tu lacérer le satin
Et boire en la salive heureuse l'inertie,

Par les cafés princiers attendre le matin?
Les plafonds enrichis de nymphes et de voiles,
On jette, au mendiant de la vitre, un festin.

Et quand tu sors, vieux dieu, grelottant sous tes toiles
D'emballage, l'aurore est un lac de vin
    d'or
Et tu jures avoir au gosier les étoiles!

Faute de supputer l'éclat de ton trésor,
Tu peux du moins t'orner d'une plume, à complies
Servir un cierge au saint en qui tu crois encor.

AUMÔNE

Take this purse, Beggar! that you did not wheedle,
senile suckling, from a stingy teat
finally to drain your knell from it little by little.

Draw from this precious metal some bizarre
and vast sin like us, whose full fists embrace it.
Blow it till it twists! a burning fanfare.

Church with incense all these houses on
the walls when, cradler of a bluish rift,
tobacco without speaking rolls orisons,

and powerful opium smashes the pharmacy!
Robes and skin! Do you want to tear the satin
and drink from spittle a happy atony,

by the princely cafés waiting for dawn to pass?
The ceilings all enriched with nymphs and veils,
a feast is tossed to the beggar before the glass.

And when you leave, old god, shivering with cold
in your gunny sacks, you'll swear you've stars in your
    gullet
and daybreak is a lake of wine of gold!

Instead of counting the splendor of your wealth,
you can sport at least a feather, at compline to serve as
candle to a saint in whom you still have faith.

Ne t'imagine pas que je dis des folies.
La terre s'ouvre vieille à qui crève la faim.
Je hais une autre aumône et veux que tu m'oublies

Et surtout ne va pas, frère, acheter du pain.

Don't fancy that I'm crazy in the head.
Earth opens old to him who dies of hunger.
I hate another alms. Think of me no longer

and above all don't go, brother, and buy any bread.

HÉRODIADE

I. Ouverture ancienne d'Hérodiade

LA NOURRICE

(Incantation)

ABOLIE, et son aile affreuse dans les larmes
Du bassin, aboli, qui mire les alarmes,
Des ors nus fustigeant l'espace cramoisi,
Une Aurore a, plumage héraldique, choisi
Notre tour cinéraire et sacrificatrice,
Lourde tombe qu'a fuie un bel oiseau, caprice
Solitaire d'aurore au vain plumage noir...
Ah! des pays déchus et tristes le manoir!
Pas de clapotement! L'eau morne se résigne,
Que ne visite plus la plume ni le cygne
Inoubliable: l'eau reflète l'abandon
De l'automne éteignant en elle son brandon:
Du cygne quand parmi le pâle mausolée
Où la plume plongea la tête, désolée
Par le diamant pur de quelque étoile, mais
Antérieure, qui ne scintilla jamais.

Crime! bûcher! aurore ancienne! supplice!
Pourpre d'un ciel! Etang de la pourpre complice!
Et sur les incarnats, grand ouvert, ce
   vitrail.

HÉRODIADE

I. Ouverture   II. Scène   III. Cantique de saint Jean

I. OUVERTURE ANCIENNE D'HÉRODIADE

LA NOURRICE

(Incantation)

ABOLISHED, and her frightful wings in the tears
of the pool, abolished, that mirrors her alarms,
the naked golds thrashing crimson space,
an Aurora has, heraldic plumage, chosen
our cinerary and sacrificial tower,
heavy tomb whence a beautiful bird has fled,
solitary caprice of dawn with vain black plumage . . .
ah, the manorhouse of sad and fallen lands!
No plashing! The gloomy water is resigned,
no longer visited by plume or swan
never forgotten: the water reflects the yielding
of autumn extinguishing therein his torch:
of the swan when amid the pallid mausoleum
where he plunged his feathery head, in grief
for the pure diamond of some star, but long
ago, a star that never scintillated.

Crime! pyre! ancient dawn! torture!
Purple of a sky! Pool of accomplice purple!
And on the rose-tints, wide-open, this stained-glass
    window.

La chambre singulière en un cadre, attirail
De siècles belliqueux, orfèvrerie éteinte,
A le neigeux jadis pour ancienne teinte,
Et sa tapisserie, au lustre nacré, plis
Inutiles avec les yeux ensevelis
De sibylles offrant leur ongle vieil aux Mages.
Une d'elles, avec un passé de ramages
Sur ma robe blanchie en l'ivoire fermé
Au ciel d'oiseaux parmi l'argent noir parsemé,
Semble, de vols partis costumée et fantôme,
Un arôme qui porte, ô roses! un arôme,
Loin du lit vide qu'un cierge soufflé cachait,
Un arôme d'os froids rôdant sur le sachet,
Une touffe de fleurs parjures à la lune,
(A la cire expirée encor s'effeuille l'une,)
De qui le long regret et les tiges de qui
Trempent en un seul verre à l'éclat alangui...
Une Aurore traînait ses ailes dans les larmes!

Ombre magicienne aux symboliques charmes!
Une voix, du passé longue évocation,
Est-ce la mienne prête à l'incantation?
Encore dans les plis jaunes de la pensée
Traînant, antique, ainsi qu'une toile encensée
Sur un confus amas d'ostensoirs refroidis,
Par les trous anciens et par les plis roidis
Percés selon le rythme et les dentelles pures
Du suaire laissant par ses belles guipures
Désespéré monter le vieil éclat voilé
S'élève; (ô quel lointain en ces appels celé!)
Le vieil éclat voilé du vermeil insolite,
De la voix languissant, nulle, sans acolyte,

The bizarre chamber in this frame, the pomp
of warring centuries, with the tarnished goldwork,
is like old snows instead of its former color,
and its tapestry, with nacrous luster, futile
folds with the shrouded eyes of sibyls offering
their aged fingernails to the Mages.
One of them, with embroideries of flowers
on my robe bleached in the closed ivory
with a sky of birds strewn on the blackened silver,
seems, garbed in risen flights and like a phantom,
an aroma reaching, O roses! an aroma,
far from the empty bed hidden by a snuffed candle,
an aroma of cold bones lingering on the sachet,
a bunch of flowers unfaithful to the moon
(by the dead candle it still sheds its petals),
flowers whose long regret and stems are steeped
in a lone vase whose brightness is bedimmed . . .
a Dawn was dragging her wings among the tears!

Sorcerer-shadow with symbolic charms!
A voice, long-drawn, evocative of the past,
(Is it mine ready for the incantation?)
languishing among the yellowed folds
of thought, and agèd as a cloth perfumed
with incense over a pile of cold church vessels,
arises through the ancient holes and through
the stiffened folds matching the rhythm and pure
lacework of the shroud that lets the desperate
old veiled brilliance mount through its meshes;
(oh, what distance hidden in these calls!)
the old veiled brilliance of a strange vermilion
of the languishing voice, toneless, without acolyte,

Jettera-t-il son or par dernières splendeurs,
Elle, encore, l'antienne aux versets demandeurs,
A l'heure d'agonie et de luttes funèbres!
Et, force du silence et des noires ténèbres
Tout rentre également en l'ancien passé,
Fatidique, vaincu, monotone, lassé,
Comme l'eau des bassins anciens se résigne.

Elle a chanté, parfois incoherente, signe
Lamentable!
            le lit aux pages de vélin,
Tel, inutile et si claustral, n'est pas le lin!
Qui des rêves par plis n'a plus le cher grimoire,
Ni le dais sépulcral à la déserte moire,
Le parfum des cheveux endormis. L'avait-il?
Froide enfant, de garder en son plaisir subtil
Au matin grelottant de fleurs, ses promenades,
Et quand le soir méchant a coupé les grenades!
Le croissant, oui le seul est au cadran de fer
De l'horloge, pour poids suspendant Lucifer,
Toujours blesse, toujours une nouvelle heurée,
Par la clepsydre à la goutte obscure pleurée,
Que, délaissée, elle erre, et sur son ombre pas
Un ange accompagnant son indicible pas!
Il ne sait pas cela le roi qui salarie
Depuis longtemps la gorge ancienne et tarie.
Son père ne sait pas cela, ni le glacier
Farouche reflétant de ses armes l'acier,
Quand sur un tas gisant de cadavres sans coffre
Odorant de résine, énigmatique, il offre
Ses trompettes d'argent obscur aux vieux sapins!

will it cast its gold among the final splendors,
still the antiphony of petitioning verses,
in the hour of agony and the death-struggles?
and, such is the power of silence and black darkness,
all return likewise to the ancient past,
monotonous, prophetic, weary, vanquished,
as the water of ancient basins grows resigned.

She has sung, sometimes incoherently,
lamentable sign!
                    the bed with vellum pages,
such, useless and so claustral, it's not linen!
No more the dear gramarye of dreams from wrinkled
sheets, the sepulchral dais with the abandoned moire,
the fragrance of sleeping hair. Did it have that?
Cold girl, to indulge her subtle pleasure
in walks at daybreak shivering with flowers
and when the spiteful evening has cut the pomegranates!
The new moon, yes the only one's on the iron
face of the clock, with Lucifer for its weight,
always wounds, always another hour,
wept by the clepsydra with its dark drops,
that she, forsaken, wanders, and on her shadow
never an angel escorts her ineffable steps!
He does not know of this, the king who pays
for this long time the dried and aged breasts.
Her father does not know this, nor the fierce
glacier reflecting the steel of armor and weapons,
when on a felled heap of corpses without coffins
odorous with resin, enigmatic, he offers
his trumpets of black silver to the old pines!

Reviendra-t-il un jour des pays cisalpins!
Assez tôt? car tout est présage et mauvais rêve!
A l'ongle qui parmi le vitrage s'élève
Selon le souvenir des trompettes, le vieux
Ciel brûle, et change un doigt en un cierge envieux.
Et bientôt sa rougeur de triste crépuscule
Pénétrera du corps la cire qui recule!
De crépuscule, non, mais de rouge lever,
Lever du jour dernier qui vient tout achever,
Si triste se débat, que l'on ne sait plus l'heure
La rougeur de ce temps prophétique qui pleure
Sur l'enfant, exilée en son cœur précieux
Comme un cygne cachant en sa plume ses yeux,
Comme les mit le vieux cygne en sa plume, allée,
De la plume détresse, en l'éternelle allée
De ses espoirs, pour voir les diamants élus
D'une étoile, mourante, et qui ne brille plus!

Will he return some day from Cisalpine lands?
Soon enough? for all is bad omens and evil dreams!
On the fingernail lifted in this stained-glass window
as if remembering the trumpets, the old sky
burns, and changes a finger to an envious taper.
And soon the red light of this sorrowful dawn
will penetrate the shrinking body of wax!
Not of dawn, no, but of the red awakening,
sunrise of the last day when all will be ended,
so sadly it struggles, one knows not the hour
the redness of this prophetic time that weeps
over the girl, exiled in her insolent heart
like a swan hiding his eyes among his plumage,
as the old swan buries them in his feathers, gone,
these rumpled feathers, in the eternal blotting
of any hope to behold the chosen diamonds
of a star, dying, and which shines no more!

II. Scene

N.

Tu vis! ou vois-je ici l'ombre d'une princesse?
A mes lèvres tes doigts et leurs bagues et
    cesse
De marcher dans un âge ignoré...

H.

              Reculez.
Le blond torrent de mes cheveux immaculés
Quand il baigne mon corps solitaire le glace
D'horreur, et mes cheveux que la lumière enlace
Sont immortels. O femme, un baiser me tûrait
Si la beauté n'était la mort...
                   Par quel attrait
Menée et quel matin oublié des prophètes
Verse, sur les lointains mourants, ses tristes fêtes,
Le sais-je? tu m'as vue, ô nourrice d'hiver,
Sous la lourde prison de pierres et de fer
Où de mes vieux lions traînent les siècles fauves
Entrer, et je marchais, fatale, les mains sauves,
Dans le parfum désert de ces anciens rois:
Mais encore as-tu vu quels furent mes effrois?
Je m'arrête rêvant aux exils, et j'effeuille
Comme près d'un bassin dont le jet d'eau m'accueille
Les pâles lys qui sont en moi, tandis qu'épris
De suivre du regard les languides débris
Descendre, à travers ma rêverie, en silence,
Les lions, de ma robe écartent l'indolence
Et regardent mes pieds qui calmeraient la mer.

28

II. Scène

N.

You're still alive! or do I see here the shade of a
    princess?
Your fingers and their rings to my lips and cease
moving in a bygone age . . .

H.

Stand back.
The flaxen torrent of my immaculate hair
when it bathes my lonely body turns it ice
with horror, and my locks enlaced with light
become immortal. O woman, a mere kiss
would kill me were not beauty death . . .

How should
I know: enticed by what spell and what morning
forgotten by prophets pours, on the dying distance,
its dreary festivals? O nurse of winter,
you have seen me go down to the massive prison
of iron and stone where my old lions draw
the tawny centuries, and I walked there, doomed,
with hands inviolable, in the desert perfume
of those former kings: but did you notice my fears?
Dreaming of banishments I stand, and I strip,
as if by a basin whose fountain welcomes me,
my pallid lilies, while the enamoured lions,
following with their gaze the languid spoils
slipping in silence through my reverie,
disregarding my robe's indolence,
watch my feet that would make calm the sea.

Calme, toi, les frissons de ta sénile chair,
Viens et ma chevelure imitant les manières
Trop farouches qui font votre peur des crinières,
Aide-moi, puisqu'ainsi tu n'oses plus me voir,
A me peigner nonchalamment dans un miroir.

N.

Sinon la myrrhe gaie en ses bouteilles closes,
De l'essence ravie aux vieillesses de roses
Voulez-vous, mon enfant, essayer la vertu
Funèbre?

H.

Laisse là ces parfums! ne sais-tu
Que je les hais, nourrice, et veux-tu que je sente
Leur ivresse noyer ma tête languissante?
Je veux que mes cheveux qui ne sont pas des fleurs
A répandre l'oubli des humaines douleurs,
Mais de l'or, à jamais vierge des aromates,
Dans leurs éclairs cruels et dans leurs pâleurs mates,
Observent la froideur stérile du métal,
Vous ayant reflétés, joyaux du mur natal,
Armes, vases depuis ma solitaire enfance.

N.

Pardon! l'âge effaçait, reine, votre défense
De mon esprit pâli comme un vieux livre ou noir...

H.

Assez! Tiens devant moi ce miroir.
                                    O miroir!
Eau froide par l'ennui dans ton cadre gelée
Que de fois et pendant des heures, désolée

Calm the shudderings of your anile flesh.
Come, and my hair imitating the manner
too ferocious that makes you afraid of manes,
help me, since you no longer dare look at me,
to comb it listlessly before a mirror.

N.

If not the cheerful myrrh in its closed bottles,
will you not try, my child, the gloomy strength
of the essence ravished from roses that are old
and faded?

H.

      Leave the perfumes! You know I hate them
Would you have me feel their intoxication drowning
my languid head? I want my hair (not flowers
diffusing oblivion on human sorrows,
but gold) forever pure of aromatics,
with its cruel lightning and dull pallor,
to be like the sterile and metallic coldness
of having reflected you, armor and vases,
gems of my natal walls from my lonely childhood.

N.

Forgive, queen! Age was blotting your command
from my memory, dim as an ancient or black book . . .

H.

Enough! Hold up this glass for me.
                  O mirror!
cold water frozen by ennui in your frame,
how many times and through what hours, distressed

Des songes et cherchant mes souvenirs qui sont
Comme des feuilles sous ta glace au trou profond,
Je m'apparus en toi comme un ombre lointaine,
Mais, horreur! des soirs, dans ta sévère fontaine,
J'ai de mon rêve épars connu la nudité!

Nourrice, suis-je belle?

N.

Un astre, en vérité
Mais cette tresse tombe...

H.

Arrête dans ton crime
Qui refroidit mon sang vers sa source, et réprime
Ce geste, impiété fameuse: ah! conte-moi
Quel sûr démon te jette en le sinistre émoi,
Ce baiser, ces parfums offerts et, le dirai-je?
O mon cœur, cette main encore sacrilège,
Car tu voulais, je crois, me toucher, sont un jour
Qui ne finira pas sans malheur sur la tour...
O jour qu'Hérodiade avec effroi regarde!

N.

Temps bizarre, en effet, de quoi le ciel vous
    garde!
Vous errez, ombre seule et nouvelle fureur,
Et regardant en vous précoce avec terreur;
Mais toujours adorable autant qu'une immortelle
O mon enfant, et belle affreusement et telle
Que...

32

by dreams and searching my memories, like leaves
under your ice in the deep hole, have I
appeared in you like a shadow far away,
but, horror! in the dusk, in your austere pool
I have known the nakedness of my scattered dreams!

Nurse, am I beautiful?

N.

Truly, a star
but this lock's slipping down . . .

H.

Restrain your crime
that chills my blood back to its source, hold back
the notorious profanation of this gesture:
ah, say what certain demon casts this sinister
emotion over you, that kiss, those perfumes
offered and, shall I say, O my heart,
this hand more sacrilegious still? because
I think you wanted to touch me—it is a day
will end on the tower not without disaster . . .
Oh, day Herodias looks on with dread!

N.

Outlandish times, indeed, from which heaven guard
 you!
You wander, solitary shade, new furor,
examining yourself, precocious with terror;
but always adorable as an immortal,
O my child, and lovely, terribly, and such
that . . .

33

H.

Mais n'allais-tu pas me toucher?

N.

... J'aimerais

Être à qui le destin réserve vos secrets.

H.

Oh! tais-toi!

N.

Viendra-t-il parfois?

H.

Etoiles pures,

N'entendez pas!

N.

Comment, sinon parmi d'obscures
Epouvantes, songer plus implacable encor
Et comme suppliant le dieu que le trésor
De votre grâce attend! et pour qui, dévorée
D'angoisses, gardez-vous la splendeur ignorée
Et le mystère vain de votre être?

H.

Pour moi.

N.

Triste fleur qui croît seule et n'a pas d'autre émoi
Que son ombre dans l'eau vue avec atonie.

H.

Va, garde ta pitié comme ton ironie.

34

H.

But were you not about to touch me?

N.

I'd love to be one for whom fate reserves your secrets.

H.

Silence!

N.

Will he come sometime?

H.

                                             Pure stars,
heed not!

N.

     How then, if not among obscure
terrors, to dream still more implacable
and like a suppliant the god for whom
your favor's treasure waits! for whom do you,
devoured by anguish, keep the unknown splendor
and the vain mystery of your being?

H.

                                                  For me.

N.

Sad flower that grows alone, not a flutter of feeling
but its shadow seen on the water languidly.

H.

Go, save your pity with your irony.

35

N.

Toutefois expliquez: oh! non, naïve enfant,
Décroîtra, quelque jour, ce dédain triomphant...

H.

Mais qui me toucherait, des lions respectée?
Du reste, je ne veux rien d'humain et, sculptée,
Si tu me vois les yeux perdus au paradis,
C'est quand je me souviens de ton lait bu jadis.

N.

Victime lamentable à son destin offerte!

H.

Oui, c'est pour moi, pour moi, que je fleuris, déserte!
Vous le savez, jardins d'améthyste, enfouis
Sans fin dans de savants abîmes éblouis,
Ors ignorés, gardant votre antique lumière
Sous le sombre sommeil d'une terre première,
Vous pierres où mes yeux comme de purs bijoux
Empruntent leur clarté mélodieuse, et vous
Métaux qui donnez à ma jeune chevelure
Une splendeur fatale et sa massive allure!
Quant à toi, femme née en des siècles malins
Pour la méchanceté des antres sibyllins,
Qui parles d'un mortel! selon qui, des calices
De mes robes, arôme aux farouches délices,
Sortirait le frisson blanc de ma nudité,
Prophétise que si le tiède azur d'été,
Vers lui nativement la femme se dévoile,
Me voit dans ma pudeur grelottante d'étoile,
Je meurs!

N.

Oh no, my naïve child! Only explain.
Some day this triumphant scorn will wane . . .

H.

But who would touch me whom the lions spared?
Besides, I want nothing human, and should you see me,
sculptured, the eyes lost in paradise,
it is when I remember your milk drunk of old.

N.

Lamentable victim offered to its doom!

H.

Yes, it's for me I bloom, for me, deserted!
You know that, amethystine gardens, hidden
without end in dazzling erudite abysses,
unknown golds, keeping your ancient light
under the somber sleep of primeval earth,
you stones from which my eyes like pure jewels
borrow their melodious clarity,
metals that give to my young locks a fatal
splendor and their flowing massive charm!
As for you, woman born in malignant times
for the wicked spitefulness of sibylline caves,
who speak of a mortal! for whom, from the chalices
of my robes, should come forth the white shuddering
of my nakedness, the aroma of fierce delights,
prophesy that if the warm azure of summer,
toward which woman instinctively unveils,
behold my shivering star of chastity,
I die!

J'aime l'horreur d'être vierge et je veux
Vivre parmi l'effroi que me font mes cheveux
Pour, le soir, retirée en ma couche, reptile
Inviolé sentir en la chair inutile
Le froid scintillement de ta pâle clarté
Toi qui te meurs, toi qui brûles de chasteté,
Nuit blanche de glaçons et de neige cruelle!

Et ta sœur solitaire, ô ma sœur éternelle
Mon rêve montera vers toi: telle déjà
Rare limpidité d'un cœur qui le songea,
Je me crois seule en ma monotone patrie
Et tout, autour de moi, vit dans l'idolâtrie
D'un miroir qui reflète en son calme dormant
Hérodiade au clair regard de diamant...
O charme dernier, oui! je le sens, je suis seule.

N.

Madame, allez-vous donc mourir?

H.

Non, pauvre aïeule,
Sois calme et, t'éloignant, pardonne à ce cœur dur,
Mais avant, si tu veux, clos les volets, l'azur
Séraphique sourit dans les vitres profondes,
Et je déteste, moi, le bel azur!

Des ondes
Se bercent et, là-bas, sais-tu pas un pays
Où le sinistre ciel ait les regards haïs
De Vénus qui, le soir, brûle dans le feuillage;
J'y partirais.

I love the horror of being virgin
and I wish to live in the terror my tresses make
thus, at evening, on my couch, a snake
inviolate, to feel in my useless flesh
the frigid scintillations of your pale glow,
you who die as yourself, who burn with chastity,
white night of icicles and cruel snow!

And your lonely sister, O my sister eternal
my dream will rise toward you: already such
rare limpidity of a heart that dreamed it,
I think I'm alone in my monotonous country,
and all, around me, lives in idolatry
of a mirror that reflects in its slumbering calm
Herodias with the lucid diamond look . . .
O supreme enchantment! I feel it, yes, I am alone.

N.

Milady, you will die then?

H.

No, poor grandam,
be calm and, leaving, pardon this hard heart,
but close the shutters first, please, for the azure
seraphically smiles in the profound panes,
and I, I hate the beautiful azure!

Yonder
the waves are tossing; if you know a land
where the sinister sky has the hateful look
of Venus burning, at evening, among the leaves,
I'd like to go there.

          Allume encore, enfantillage
Dis-tu, ces flambeaux où la cire au feu léger
Pleure parmi l'or vain quelque pleur étranger
Et...

                    N.

   Maintenant?

                    H.

          Adieu.
                    Vous mentez, ô fleur nue
De mes lèvres.
                    J'attends une chose inconnue
Ou peut-être, ignorant le mystère et vos cris,
Jetez-vous les sanglots suprêmes et meurtris
D'une enfance sentant parmi les rêveries
Se séparer enfin ses froides pierreries.

And though you say it's childish,
kindle those links where wax with frivolous fire
weeps an alien tear in the vain gold
and . . .

N.

And now?

H.

Farewell.
O naked flower
of my lips, you lie!
I await a thing unknown
or perhaps, unaware of the mystery and your cries
you give, O lips, the supreme tortured moans
of a childhood groping among its reveries
to sort out finally its cold precious stones.

III. Cantique de saint Jean

Le soleil que sa halte
Surnaturelle exalte
Aussitôt redescend
   Incandescent

Je sens comme aux vertèbres
S'éployer des ténèbres
Toutes dans un frisson
   A l'unisson

Et ma tête surgie
Solitaire vigie
Dans les vols triomphaux
   De cette faux

Comme rupture franche
Plutôt refoule ou tranche
Les anciens désaccords
   Avec le corps

Qu'elle de jeûnes ivre
S'opiniâtre à suivre
En quelque bond hagard
   Son pur regard

Là-haut où la froidure
Eternelle n'endure
Que vous le surpassiez
   Tous ô glaciers

III. Cantique de saint Jean

THE sun that is exalted
by its supernatural halt
forthwith redescends
   incandescent

I feel how vertebrae
in the dark give way
all of them together
   in a shudder

and in lonely vigil
among flights triumphal
of this scythe's swings
   my head springs

as the downright rupture
represses or cuts rather
the primordial clash
   with the flesh

Drunken with abstinence
may it stubbornly advance
in some haggard flight
   its pure sight

up where the infinite
cold does not permit
that you be its surpassers
   O all glaciers

43

Mais selon un baptême
Illuminée au même
Principe qui m'élut
    Penche un salut.

.

but, thanks to a baptism
shining from the chrism
of that consecration
  my head bows salutation.

L'APRÈS-MIDI D'UN FAUNE

Églogue

LE FAUNE

Ces nymphes, je les veux perpétuer.

                                        Si clair,
Leur incarnat léger, qu'il voltige dans l'air
Assoupi de sommeils touffus.

                              Aimai-je un rêve?
Mon doute, amas de nuit ancienne, s'achève
En maint rameau subtil, qui, demeuré les vrais
Bois mêmes, prouve, hélas! que bien seul je m'offrais
Pour triomphe la faute idéale de roses.
Réfléchissons...

                  ou si les femmes dont tu gloses
Figurent un souhait de tes sens fabuleux!
Faune, l'illusion s'échappe des yeux bleus
Et froids, comme une source en pleurs, de la plus chaste:
Mais, l'autre tout soupirs, dis-tu qu'elle contraste
Comme brise du jour chaude dans ta toison?
Que non! par l'immobile et lasse pâmoison
Suffoquant de chaleurs le matin frais s'il lutte,
Ne murmure point d'eau que ne verse ma flûte
Au bosquet arrosé d'accords; et le seul vent
Hors des deux tuyaux prompt à s'exhaler avant
Qu'il disperse le son dans une pluie aride,
C'est, à l'horizon pas remué d'une ride,
Le visible et serein souffle artificiel
De l'inspiration, qui regagne le ciel.

46

L'APRÈS-MIDI D'UN FAUNE

Églogue

LE FAUNE

I WOULD perpetuate these nymphs.

So clear,
their light carnation, that it drifts on the air
drowsy with tufted slumbers.

So I loved a dream?
My doubt, a mass of ancient night, concludes
in many a subtle branch, which, since the real woods
remain, proves, alas, what I offered to myself
as triumph was the ideal lack of roses.
Let's think it over . . .

if those girls you explain
be but an itching in your fabulous brain!
Faun, the illusion escapes from the blue eyes
and cold of the more chaste, like a weeping spring:
but the other one, all sighs, you say, contrasts
like a day-breeze warm upon your fleece!
But no! through the immobile and heavy swoon
stifling with heat the cool morning if it resists,
murmurs no water but that poured from my flute
on the grove sprinkled with harmonies; the only wind
prompt to exhale from the twin-pipes before
it can disperse the sound in an arid rain,
is, on the horizon unstirred by a wrinkle,
the visible and serene artificial breath
of inspiration, which regains the sky.

O bords siciliens d'un calme marécage
Qu'à l'envi des soleils ma vanité saccage,
Tacite sous les fleurs d'étincelles, CONTEZ
"Que je coupais ici les creux roseaux domptés
Par le talent; quand, sur l'or glauque de lointaines
Verdures dédiant leur vigne à des fontaines,
Ondoie une blancheur animale au repos:
Et qu'au prélude lent où naissent les pipeaux
Ce vol de cygnes, non! de naïades se sauve
Ou plonge..."

          Inerte, tout brûle dans l'heure fauve
Sans marquer par quel art ensemble détala
Trop d'hymen souhaité de qui cherche le *la:*
Alors m'éveillerai-je à la ferveur première,
Droit et seul, sous un flot antique de lumière,
Lys! et l'un de vous tous pour l'ingénuité.

Autre que ce doux rien par leur lèvre ébruité,
Le baiser, qui tout bas des perfides
    assure,
Mon sein, vierge de preuve, atteste une morsure
Mystérieuse, due à quelque auguste dent;
Mais, bast! arcane tel élut pour confident
Le jonc vaste et jumeau dont sous l'azur on joue:
Qui, détournant à soi le trouble de la joue
Rêve, dans un solo long, que nous amusions
La beauté d'alentour pas des confusions
Fausses entre elle-même et notre chant crédule;
Et de faire aussi haut que l'amour se module
Evanouir du songe ordinaire de dos
Ou de flanc pur suivis avec mes regards clos,
Une sonore, vaine et monotone ligne.

O Sicilian borders of a peaceful marsh
which like unto the sun my vanity plunders,
tacit under the flowers of sparks, RELATE
"How I was cutting here the hollow reeds
tamed by my talent; when, on the glaucous gold
of distant verdures dedicating their vines
to the fountains, undulated an animal whiteness,
reposing: and to the slow prelude whence the pipes
are born, this flight of swans, no! of Naiades
goes scampering off or dives . . ."

                                    Inert, all things
burn in the tawny hour, not noticing
by what art together fled this too much hymen
desired by who seeks for *la:* then I'll awaken
to the primal fervor, erect and alone,
under the antique flood of light, O lilies!
and the one among you all for artlessness.

Besides this sweet nothing by their lips made known,
the kiss, that reveals, though hushed, some faithless
    ones,
my breast, virgin of proof, vouches a bite,
mysterious, from some illustrious tooth;
but enough! as confidant such arcanum chose
the great twin-reeds one plays beneath the azure:
which, diverting to themselves the cheeks' excitement,
dream, in a long solo, that we may amuse
the beauties hereabout by false confusions
between them even and our credulous song;
and to make as high as love can modulate
vanish from the banal dream of backs
or pure flanks pursued in my closed eyes,
a sonorous and vain, monotonous line.

Tâche donc, instrument des fuites, ô maligne
Syrinx, de refleurir aux lacs où tu m'attends!
Moi, de ma rumeur fier, je vais parler longtemps
Des déesses; et par d'idolâtres peintures,
A leur ombre enlever encore des ceintures:
Ainsi, quand des raisins j'ai sucé la clarté,
Pour bannir un regret par ma feinte écarté,
Rieur, j'élève au ciel d'été la grappe vide
Et, soufflant dans ses peaux lumineuses, avide
D'ivresse, jusqu'au soir je regarde au travers.

O nymphes, regonflons des SOUVENIRS divers.
"Mon œil, trouant les joncs, dardait chaque encolure
Immortelle, qui noie en l'onde sa brûlure
Avec un cri de rage au ciel de la forêt;
Et le splendide bain de cheveux disparaît
Dans les clartés et les frissons, ô pierreries!
J'accours; quand, à mes pieds, s'entrejoignent (meur-
    tries
De la langueur goûtée à ce mal d'être deux)
Des dormeuses parmi leurs seuls bras hasardeux;
Je les ravis, sans les désenlacer, et vole
A ce massif, haï par l'ombrage frivole,
De roses tarissant tout parfum au soleil,
Où notre ébat au jour consumé soit pareil."
Je t'adore, courroux des vierges, ô délice
Farouche du sacré fardeau nu qui se glisse
Pour fuir ma lèvre en feu buvant, comme un éclair
Tressaille! le frayeur secrète de la chair:
Des pieds de l'inhumaine au cœur de la
    timide
Que délaisse à la fois une innocence, humide
De larmes folles ou de moins tristes vapeurs.

Try then, instrument of flights, O evil
Syrinx, to flower again by the lakes where you wait!
Proud of my noise, I am going to talk at length
of the goddesses; and by idolatrous paintings
to lift again the cinctures from their shadows:
so, when I have sucked the bright juice of the grapes,
to banish a regret by my pretense discarded,
laughing, I raise to the summer sky the empty
hulls and, puffing into these luminous skins,
craving drunkenness, I gaze through them till evening.

O nymphs, we swell with divers MEMORIES.
"Piercing the reeds, my eyes speared each immortal
neck, that drowns its burning in the water
with a cry of rage flung to the forest sky;
and the splendid bath of tresses disappeared
in shimmerings and shiverings, O jewels!
I rush up; when, at my feet, entwine
    (bruised
by the languor drunk from this harm of being two)
girls sleeping in each other's perilous arms;
I seize them, not untangling them, and run
to this clump, hated by the frivolous shade,
of roses exhausting all their scent in the sun,
where our frolic should be like a squandered day."
I adore you, anger of virgins, O fierce delight
of the sacred naked burden that slips to flee
the fiery drinking of my lips, like the crack
of lightning! the secret terror of the flesh:
from the feet of the heartless one to the heart of the
    timid
abandoned at the same time by an innocence, humid
with foolish tears or less melancholy vapors.

"Mon crime, c'est d'avoir, gai de vaincre ces peurs
Traîtresses, divisé la touffe échevelée
De baisers que les dieux gardaient si bien mêlée:
Car, à peine j'allais cacher un rire ardent
Sous les replis heureux d'une seule (gardant
Par un doigt simple, afin que sa candeur de plume
Se teignît à l'émoi de sa sœur qui s'allume,
La petite, naïve et ne rougissant pas:)
Que de mes bras, défaits par de vagues trépas,
Cette proie, à jamais ingrate se délivre
Sans pitié du sanglot dont j'étais encore ivre."

Tant pis! vers le bonheur d'autres m'entraîneront
Par leur tresse nouée aux cornes de mon front:
Tu sais, ma passion, que, pourpre et déjà mûre,
Chaque grenade éclate et d'abeilles murmure;
Et notre sang, épris de qui le va saisir,
Coule pour tout l'essaim éternel du désir.
A l'heure où ce bois d'or et de cendres se
    teinte
Une fête s'exalte en la feuillée éteinte:
Etna! c'est parmi toi visité de Vénus
Sur ta lave posant ses talons ingénus,
Quand tonne un somme triste ou s'épuise la flamme.
Je tiens la reine!

        O sûr châtiment...

                  Non, mais l'âme
De paroles vacante et ce corps alourdi
Tard succombent au fier silence de midi:

"My crime is, gay at vanquishing their traitress-
fears, to have parted the disheveled tangle
of kisses that the gods kept so well mingled;
for I was just going to hide a glowing laugh
in the happy creases of one (even while I kept
with only a finger—so that her plume's candor
should be stained by the frenzy of her sister
who burned—the little one, naïve, not blushing a bit:)
when from my arms, relaxed by the vague death,
this prey, forever ungrateful, frees itself,
not pitying the sob that still bedrunkened me."

Too bad! but others will lead me toward happiness,
knotting the horns on my brow with many a tress;
you know, my passion, how, crimson and already ripe,
every pomegranate bursts and murmurs with bees;
and our blood, burning for who is going to receive it,
flows for all the eternal swarm of desire.
At the hour when this wood is stained with gold and
     ashes
a feast exults among extinguished leaves:
Etna! it is on you visited by Venus
upon your lava setting her candid feet
when thunders a sad slumber or the flame expires.
I embrace the queen!

                    Sure punishment . . .

                                   No, but the spirit
empty of words now and the body numbed
unto noon's haughty silence at last succumb:

Sans plus il faut dormir en l'oubli du blasphème,
Sur le sable altéré gisant et comme j'aime
Ouvrir ma bouche à l'astre efficace des vins!

Couple, adieu; je vais voir l'ombre que tu devins.

enough! on the thirsty sand, forgetful of
the outrage, I must sleep, and as I love
open my mouth to the powerful star of wine!

Sweet pair, farewell. I shall see the shades you become.

SAINTE

A LA fenêtre recélant
Le santal vieux qui se dédore
De sa viole étincelant
Jadis avec flûte ou mandore,

Est la Sainte pâle, étalant
Le livre vieux qui se déplie
Du Magnificat ruisselant
Jadis selon vêpre et complie:

A ce vitrage d'ostensoir
Que frôle une harpe par l'Ange
Formée avec son vol du soir
Pour la délicate phalange

Du doigt que, sans le vieux santal
Ni le vieux livre, elle balance
Sur le plumage instrumental,
Musicienne du silence.

SAINTE

AT THE window concealing
the old sandalwood lute
that once, its gilt is peeling,
shone with mandora or flute

is the pale Saint, showing
the old book outspread
at the Magnificat glowing
once for services read;

at this stained-glass window lightly
touched by a harp shaped
by the Angel in evening flight
for the delicate finger-tip

that, without the old santal
or the old book, she balances
on the plumage instrumental,
musician of silence.

TOAST FUNÈBRE

O DE notre bonheur, toi, le fatal emblème!

Salut de la démence et libation blême,
Ne crois pas qu'au magique espoir du corridor
J'offre ma coupe vide où souffre un monstre d'or!
Ton apparition ne va pas me suffire:
Car je t'ai mis, moi-même, en un lieu de porphyre.
Le rite est pour les mains d'éteindre le
    flambeau
Contre le fer épais des portes du tombeau:
Et l'on ignore mal, élu pour notre fête
Très simple de chanter l'absence du poète,
Que ce beau monument l'enferme tout entier.
Si ce n'est que la gloire ardente du métier,
Jusqu'à l'heure commune et vile de la cendre,
Par le carreau qu'allume un soir fier d'y descendre,
Retourne vers les feux du pur soleil mortel!

Magnifique, total et solitaire, tel
Tremble de s'exhaler le faux orgueil des hommes.
Cette foule hagarde! elle annonce: Nous sommes
La triste opacité de nos spectres futurs.
Mais le blason des deuils épars sur de vains murs
J'ai méprisé l'horreur lucide d'une larme,
Quand, sourd même à mon vers sacré qui ne l'alarme
Quelqu'un de ces passants, fier, aveugle et muet,
Hôte de son linceul vague, se transmuait
En le vierge héros de l'attente posthume.
Vaste gouffre apporté dans l'amas de la brume
Par l'irascible vent des mots qu'il n'a pas dits,
Le néant à cet Homme aboli de jadis:

TOAST FUNÈBRE

O FATAL emblem of our happiness!

Pale libation and a toast to madness,
think not to the magic hope of the corridor
I offer my empty cup where a gold monster suffers!
Your apparition is not enough for me:
for I myself put you in a place of porphyry.
In accord with the rites our hands must quench the
  torch
against the thick iron doors of the tomb's porch:
all know well, chosen for our so simple fête
to sing the poet's absence, that in this great
monument the whole of him is laid:
unless the blazing glory of his trade,
until the vile and common hour of cinders,
through panes lit by an evening proud to descend there,
return to the fires of the pure mortal sun!

Magnificent, whole and solitary, this one,
such that man's false pride trembles to breathe it out.
This haggard crowd announces: We are but
the sad opacity of our future specters.
But I have scorned the blazon of mourning scattered
on vain walls, the lucid horror of a tear,
when, deaf to my sacred verse that he does not fear,
one of these passers-by, proud, blind and mute,
guest of his vague cerements, was transmuted
as the virginal hero of posthumous delays.
Vast vortex borne amid a mass of haze
by the angry wind of words that he did not say,
zero to this Man abolished yesterday:

"Souvenirs d'horizons, qu'est-ce, ô toi, que la Terre?"
Hurle ce songe; et, voix dont la clarté s'altère,
L'espace a pour jouet le cri: "Je ne sais pas!"

Le Maître, par un œil profond, a, sur ses pas,
Apaisé de l'éden l'inquiète merveille
Dont le frisson final, dans sa voix seule, éveille
Pour la Rose et le Lys le mystère d'un nom.
Est-il de ce destin rien qui demeure, non?
O vous tous, oubliez une croyance sombre.
Le splendide génie éternel n'a pas d'ombre.
Moi, de votre désir soucieux, je veux voir,
A qui s'évanouit, hier, dans le devoir
Idéal que nous font les jardins de cet astre,
Survivre pour l'honneur du tranquille désastre
Une agitation solennelle par l'air
De paroles, pourpre ivre et grand calice clair,
Que, pluie et diamant, le regard diaphane
Resté là sur ces fleurs dont nulle ne se fane,
Isole parmi l'heure et le rayon du jour!

C'est de nos vrais bosquets déjà tout le séjour,
Où le poëte pur a pour geste humble et large
De l'interdire au rêve, ennemi de sa charge:
Afin que le matin de son repos altier,
Quand la mort ancienne est comme pour Gautier
De n'ouvrir pas les yeux sacrés et de se taire,
Surgisse, de l'allée ornement tributaire,
Le sépulcre solide où gît tout ce qui nuit,
Et l'avare silence et la massive nuit.

"What is the Earth, O memories of horizons?"
yells this dream; and, voice whose clarity lessens,
space has for a toy the cry: "I do not know!"

The Master, with his eyes profound bent low,
appeased, as he went, the troubled marvel of Eden
whose final shudder, in his voice only, wakens
for the Rose and the Lily the mystery of a name.
No! nothing of this destiny remains.
O all of you, forget so drab a creed.
Genius, eternal and glorious, has no shade.
As you desire, I would see, for this one
(yesterday, to the ideal duty gone,
assigned for us by the gardens of this star)
survive for the honor of the tranquil disaster
a solemn agitation of words through the air,
drunken crimson, a chalice large and clear,
that, rain and diamonds, the diaphanous gaze,
fixed on these flowers of which not one decays,
isolates in the hour and radiance of day!

Of our true groves already the one stay,
where the pure poet wholly, humbly must
interdict the dream, enemy of his trust:
so that of his exalted rest the day
when ancient death is as for Gautier
not to open his sacred eyes and to keep still,
may arise, tribute and ornament of this aisle,
the solid tomb where lie all harm and blight,
and miserly silence and the massive night.

PROSE

pour des Esseintes

HYPERBOLE! de ma mémoire
Triomphalement ne sais-tu
Te lever, aujourd'hui grimoire
Dans un livre de fer vêtu:

Car j'installe, par la science,
L'hymne des cœurs spirituels
En l'œuvre de ma patience,
Atlas, herbiers et rituels.

Nous promenions notre visage
(Nous fûmes deux, je le maintiens)
Sur maints charmes de paysage,
O sœur, y comparant les tiens.

L'ère d'autorité se trouble
Lorsque, sans nul motif, on dit
De ce midi que notre double
Inconscience approfondit

Que, sol des cent iris, son site,
Ils savent s'il a bien été,
Ne porte pas de nom que cite
L'or de la trompette d'Eté.

Oui, dans une île que l'air charge
De vue et non de visions
Toute fleur s'étalait plus large
Sans que nous en devisions.

PROSE

pour des Esseintes

HYPERBOLE! from my memory
triumphant can you not arise,
today from a book bound with iron
as cabalistic gramaries:

because by knowledge I induct
the hymn of all hearts spirituel
to this labor of my patience,
atlas, herbal, ritual.

We would turn our visages
(I maintain that we were two),
O sister, to the landscape's charms,
always comparing them with you.

The era of authority
is troubled when, with no motifs,
they say of this southland our double
mind's subconsciousness perceives

that, hundred-iris bed, its site,
they know if really it existed,
does not bear a name the gold
of the Summer's trumpet cited.

Yes, on an island charged by air
not with visions but with sight
every flower showed off, freer,
though we never spoke of it.

63

Telles, immenses, que chacune
Ordinairement se para
D'un lucide contour, lacune
Qui des jardins la sépara.

Gloire du long désir, Idées
Tout en moi s'exaltait de voir
La famille des iridées
Surgir à ce nouveau devoir,

Mais cette sœur sensée et tendre
Ne porta son regard plus loin
Que sourire et, comme à l'entendre
J'occupe mon antique soin.

Oh! sache l'Esprit de litige,
A cette heure où nous nous taisons,
Que de lis multiples la tige
Grandissait trop pour nos raisons

Et non comme pleure la rive,
Quand son jeu monotone ment
A vouloir que l'ampleur arrive
Parmi mon jeune étonnement

D'ouïr tout le ciel et la carte
Sans fin attestés sur mes pas,
Par le flot même qui s'écarte,
Que ce pays n'exista pas.

L'enfant abdique son extase
Et docte déjà par chemins

Such, immense, that every one
usually adorned itself
with a lucid edge, lacuna
which from the gardens set it off.

Glory of long desire, Ideas
all in me with great elation
saw the family Irides
arise to this new consecration,

but this sensible fond sister
went no further than to spare
a smile and, to understand her,
I attend my ancient care.

O Spirit of contention! know
at this hour when we are still,
that too tall for reason grows
the stalk of multiple asphodels

and not as the shore weeps,
when its monotonous frolic lies
to wish an amplitude would come
into my juvenile surprise

at hearing all the sky and map
always in my steps attested,
by the wave even that ebbs away,
that this country never existed.

Already lessoned by the roads
the child resigns her ecstasy

65

Elle dit le mot: Anastase!
Né pour d'éternels parchemins,

Avant qu'un sépulcre ne rie
Sous aucun climat, son aïeul,
De porter ce nom: Pulchérie!
Caché par le trop grand glaïeul.

and says it: Anastasius! born
for parchments of eternity,

before a sepulcher could laugh
in any clime, her ancestor,
to bear the name: Pulcheria!
hidden by the too great lily's flower.

AUTRE ÉVENTAIL

de Mademoiselle Mallarmé

O RÊVEUSE, pour que je plonge
Au pur délice sans chemin,
Sache, par un subtil mensonge,
Garder mon aile dans ta main.

Une fraîcheur de crépuscule
Te vient à chaque battement
Dont le coup prisonnier recule
L'horizon délicatement.

Vertige! voici que frissonne
L'espace comme un grand baiser
Qui, fou de naître pour personne,
Ne peut jaillir ni s'apaiser.

Sens-tu le paradis farouche
Ainsi qu'un rire enseveli
Se couler du coin de ta bouche
Au fond de l'unanime pli!

Le sceptre des rivages roses
Stagnants sur les soirs d'or, ce l'est,
Ce blanc vol fermé que tu poses
Contre le feu d'un bracelet.

AUTRE ÉVENTAIL

de Mademoiselle Mallarmé

O DREAMER, that I may dive
in pure pathless delight, understand
how subtly to connive
to keep my wing in your hand.

A coolness of twilight is sent
over you by each imprisoned
flutter whose beat extends
delicately the horizon.

Vertigo! how space quakes
like a great kiss, wild
to be born for no one's sake,
but can neither spring nor be stilled.

Do you feel the fierce paradise
like stifled laughter that slips
from the corner of your lips
to the deep unanimous crease?

The scepter of shores of rose
stagnant on evenings of gold, it's
this white closed flight you pose
against the fire of a bracelet.

FEUILLET D'ALBUM

Tout à coup et comme par jeu
Mademoiselle qui voulûtes
Ouïr se révéler un peu
Le bois de mes diverses flûtes

Il me semble que cet essai
Tenté devant un paysage
A du bon quand je le cessai
Pour vous regarder au visage

Oui ce vain souffle que j'exclus
Jusqu'à la dernière limite
Selon mes quelques doigts perclus
Manque de moyens s'il imite

Votre très naturel et clair
Rire d'enfant qui charme l'air.

FEUILLET D'ALBUM

OF A sudden and as if for fun
Mademoiselle who wanted
to hear revealed the tone
my several wood-winds fluted

it seems to me this test
tried in a scenic place
was better when I ceased
so I could gaze at your face

Yes this vain denied whiff
up to the last notch
allowed by my somewhat stiff
fingers lacks means to match

your so childish natural clear
laughter that charms the air.

REMÉMORATION D'AMIS BELGES

A DES heures et sans que tel souffle l'émeuve
Toute la vétusté presque couleur encens
Comme furtive d'elle et visible je sens
Que se dévêt pli selon pli la pierre veuve

Flotte ou semble par soi n'apporter une preuve
Sinon d'épandre pour baume antique le temps
Nous immémoriaux quelques-uns si contents
Sur la soudaineté de notre amitié neuve

O très chers rencontrés en le jamais banal
Bruges multipliant l'aube au défunt canal
Avec la promenade éparse de maint cygne

Quand solennellement cette cité m'apprit
Lesquels entre ses fils un autre vol désigne
A prompte irradier ainsi qu'aile l'esprit.

REMÉMORATION D'AMIS BELGES

SOMETIMES and without such a rousing puff
all the decrepitude (almost color of incense
as furtively and visibly I sense
how fold by fold the widowed stone strips off)

wavers or seems in itself without evidence
except to spread, like healing balm, the time
when we immemorial someones (were) so content
with the suddenness of our new friendship's prime

O very dear ones met in this never banal
Bruges multiplying the dawn on the defunct canal
with the scattered promenade of many swans

when solemnly this city among its sons
showed me those whom another flight designs
to irradiate swiftly what the spirit wings.

CHANSONS BAS

III

Le Cantonnier

Ces cailloux, tu les nivelles
Et c'est, comme troubadour,
Un cube aussi de cervelles
Qu'il me faut ouvrir par jour.

IV

Le Marchand d'ail et d'oignons

L'ennui d'aller en visite
Avec l'ail nous l'éloignons.
L'élégie au pleur hésite
Peu si je fends des oignons.

V

La Femme de l'ouvrier

La femme, l'enfant, la soupe
En chemin pour le carrier
Le complimentent qu'il coupe
Dans l'us de se marier.

VII

Le Crieur d'imprimés

Toujours, n'importe le titre,
Sans même s'enrhumer au
Dégel, ce gai siffle-litre
Crie un premier numéro.

CHANSONS BAS

III

LE CANTONNIER

You level stones in the lane;
as a troubadour, in the same way,
it's also a cube of the brain
that I must crack up every day.

IV

LE MARCHAND D'AIL ET D'OIGNONS

A clove of garlic can keep
off the boredom of a call.
With onions cut small
an elegy's easy to weep.

V

LA FEMME DE L'OUVRIER

The wife, child, and soup pot
along the road to the quarry
buck up a guy till he's got
himself in the notion to marry.

VII

LE CRIEUR D'IMPRIMÉS

Always, no matter what caption,
even in March without sniffles,
this gay half-pint whistles
and yells out the first edition.

LA MARCHANDE D'HABITS

Le vif œil dont tu regardes
Jusques à leur contenu
Me sépare de mes hardes
Et comme un dieu je vais nu.

La Marchande d'habits

The lively eyes that prod
the contents of my clothes
shuck me out of those
and I go bare as a god.

PETIT AIR

I

Quelconque une solitude
Sans le cygne ni le quai
Mire sa désuétude
Au regard que j'abdiquai

Ici de la gloriole
Haute à ne la pas toucher
Dont maint ciel se bariole
Avec les ors de coucher

Mais langoureusement longe
Comme de blanc linge ôté
Tel fugace oiseau si plonge
Exultatrice à côté

Dans l'onde toi devenue
Ta jubilation nue.

II

Indomptablement a dû
Comme mon espoir s'y lance
Eclater là-haut perdu
Avec furie et silence,

Voix étrangère au bosquet
Ou par nul écho suivie,
L'oiseau qu'on n'ouït jamais
Une autre fois en la vie.

PETIT AIR

JUST any solitude
with neither swan nor dock
mirrors its desuetude
in my abdicated look

Here from the affectation
too high to be won
of many a sky's striation
with the golds of setting sun

but langourously skims off
like white linen doffed
some transient bird if dives
(at my side in exultation

in the wave thus made alive)
your naked jubilation.

II

Indomitably must
as there my hopes rush
burst on high lost
in fury and hush,

voice strange to the wood,
without echo, the bird
that never more could
in life be heard.

La hagard musicien,
Cela dans le doute expire
Si de mon sein pas du sien
A jailli le sanglot pire

Déchiré va-t-il entier
Rester sur quelque sentier!

Wild singer, this
one dying in doubt
if from my breast not his
the worse sob gushed out

All torn will he stay
on some pathway?

PLUSIEURS SONNETS

II

Le vierge, le vivace et le bel aujourd'hui
Va-t-il nous déchirer avec un coup d'aile ivre
Ce lac dur oublié que hante sous le givre
Le transparent glacier des vols qui n'ont pas fui!

Un cygne d'autrefois se souvient que c'est lui
Magnifique mais qui sans espoir se délivre
Pour n'avoir pas chanté la région où vivre
Quand du stérile hiver a resplendi l'ennui.

Tout son col secouera cette blanche agonie
Par l'espace infligée à l'oiseau qui le nie,
Mais non l'horreur du sol où le plumage
    est pris.

Fantôme qu'à ce lieu son pur éclat assigne,
Il s'immobilise au songe froid de mépris
Que vêt parmi l'exil inutile le Cygne.

III

Victorieusement fui le suicide beau
Tison de gloire, sang par écume, or, tempête!
O rire si là-bas une pourpre s'apprête
A ne tendre royal que mon absent tombeau.

Quoi! de tout cet éclat pas même le lambeau
S'attarde, il est minuit, à l'ombre qui nous fête
Excepté qu'un trésor présomptueux de tête
Verse son caressé nonchaloir sans flambeau,

PLUSIEURS SONNETS

II

THE lively, lovely and virginal today
will its drunken wings tear for us with a blow
this lake hard and forgotten, haunted below
the frost by the clear glacier of flights not made?

A swan of past times remembers he's the one
magnificent but striving without hope
for not having sung a land where he could stop
when the ennui of sterile winter has shone.

All his neck will shake off this white death by space
inflicted on the bird for whom it is not,
but never the horror of clay where his feathers are
    caught.

Phantom whose pure white dooms it to this place,
swathed in futile exile with a chill
dream of contumely, the Swan is still.

III

Victoriously fled the grand suicide
firebrand of glory, storm, gold, blood in foam!
Oh to laugh if there below a purple is spread
to invest royally only my absent tomb.

What! not even a scrap of all the splendor
is left, it's midnight, in our festive shade
except that a presumptive treasure of head
pours without a torch its fondled languor,

La tienne si toujours le délice! la tienne
Oui seule qui du ciel évanoui retienne
Un peu de puéril triomphe en t'en coiffant

Avec clarté quand sur les coussins tu la poses
Comme un casque guerrier d'impératrice enfant
Dont pour te figurer il tomberait des roses.

IV

Ses purs ongles très haut dédiant leur onyx,
L'Angoisse, ce minuit, soutient, lampadophore,
Maint rêve vespéral brûlé par le Phénix
Que ne recueille pas de cinéraire amphore

Sur les crédences, au salon vide: nul ptyx,
Aboli bibelot d'inanité sonore,
(Car le Maître est allé puiser des pleurs au Styx
Avec ce seul objet dont le Néant s'honore).

Mais proche la croisée au nord vacante, un or
Agonise selon peut-être le décor
Des licornes ruant du feu contre une nixe,

Elle, défunte nue en le miroir, encor
Que, dans l'oubli fermé par le cadre, se fixe
De scintillations sitôt le septuor.

yours always so delightful! yes, it's yours
alone retaining of the vanished sky
a bit of childish triumph as you make lie

shining on the cushions every tress
like the warrior-helmet of a child-empress
from which to denote you roses would pour.

IV

Her pure nails very high dedicating their onyx,
Anguish, this midnight, supports a torch where burns
many a vesperal dream consumed by the Phoenix
which is not collected in the cinereal urn

on the credenzas, in the bare room: no ptyx,
abolished bibelot empty and sonorous
(for the Master has gone to draw tears from the Styx
with the sole object by which the Nothing is honored).

But near the window open on the north
a gold is dying perhaps in the décor
of unicorns kicking fire at a nixie,

who, defunct and nude in the mirror, as yet
in the oblivion bound by the frame, is fixed
of scintillations forthwith the septet.

SONNET

(Pour votre chère morte, son ami)   2 *novembre* 1877

—"Sur les bois oubliés quand passe l'hiver sombre
Tu te plains, ô captif solitaire du seuil,
Que ce sépulcre à deux qui fera notre orgueil
Hélas! du manque seul des lourds bouquets s'encombre.

Sans écouter Minuit qui jeta son vain nombre,
Une veille t'exalte à ne pas fermer l'œil
Avant que dans les bras de l'ancien fauteuil
Le suprême tison n'ait éclairé mon Ombre.

Qui veut souvent avoir la Visite ne doit
Par trop de fleurs charger la pierre que mon doigt
Soulève avec l'ennui d'une force défunte.

Ame au si clair foyer tremblante de m'asseoir,
Pour revivre il suffit qu'à tes lèvres j'emprunte
Le souffle de mon nom murmuré tout un soir."

SONNET

(Pour votre chère morte, son ami)   **2 novembre 1877**

—"WHEN on the forgotten wood dark winter passes
you mourn, O lonely captive of the sill,
that this double tomb to be our pride is ill
laden, alas, with the lack of heavy posies.

"Unheard by you Midnight's vain tale is cast,
a vigil exalts you not to close a lid
till sunken in the old armchair the last
ember has illuminated my Shade.

"Who would have the Visit often should not weight
with too many flowers the stone my finger heaves
with the weariness of a defunctive force.

"Soul trembling to seat myself by the so bright grate,
that I live again the borrowed breaths suffice
from your lips murmuring my name all the evening."

LE TOMBEAU D'EDGAR POE

Tel qu'en Lui-même enfin l'éternité le change,
Le Poëte suscite avec un glaive nu
Son siècle épouvanté de n'avoir pas connu
Que la mort triomphait dans cette voix étrange!

Eux, comme un vil sursaut d'hydre oyant jadis l'ange
Donner un sens plus pur aux mots de la tribu
Proclamèrent très haut le sortilège bu
Dans le flot sans honneur de quelque noir mélange.

Du sol et de la nue hostiles, ô grief!
Si notre idée avec ne sculpte un bas-relief
Dont la tombe de Poe éblouissante s'orne,

Calme bloc ici-bas chu d'un désastre obscur,
Que ce granit du moins montre à jamais sa borne
Aux noirs vols du Blasphème épars dans le futur.

LE TOMBEAU D'EDGAR POE

Such as into Himself at last eternity changes
him, the Poet stirs with a naked sword
his century dismayed to have ignored
that death still triumphed in this voice so strange!

With a hydra-spasm, once hearing the angel endow
with a sense more pure the words of the tribe,
they loudly proclaimed the sortilege imbibed
from the dishonorable flood of some black brew.

Alas, from the warring heaven and earth, if
our concept cannot carve a bas-relief
with which to adorn Poe's dazzling sepulcher,

calm block fallen down here from some dark
disaster, let this granite forever mark
bounds to dark flights of Blasphemy scarce in the future.

LE TOMBEAU DE CHARLES BAUDELAIRE

Le temple enseveli divulgue par la bouche
Sépulcrale d'égout bavant boue et rubis
Abominablement quelque idole Anubis
Tout le museau flambé comme un aboi farouche

Ou que le gaz récent torde la mèche louche
Essuyeuse on le sait des opprobres subis
Il allume hagard un immortel pubis
Dont le vol selon le réverbère découche

Quel feuillage séché dans les cités sans soir
Votif pourra bénir comme elle se rasseoir
Contre le marbre vainement de Baudelaire

Au voile qui la ceint absente avec frissons
Celle son Ombre même un poison tutélaire
Toujours à respirer si nous en périssons.

LE TOMBEAU DE CHARLES BAUDELAIRE

THE buried temple reveals by the sewer's dark
sepulchral mouth slavering mud and rubies
abominably some idol of Anubis
all the muzzle flaming like a ferocious bark

or if the recent gas twists a squinting wick
that puts up with who knows what dubious
disgrace it haggardly lights an immortal pubis
whose flight depends on the streetlamp to stay awake

What dried wreaths in cities without evening
votively could bless as if could sit
vainly against the marble of Baudelaire

(in the veil that clothes the absent with shudderings)
this his Shade even a poison tutelar
ever to be breathed though we die of it.

TOMBEAU

Anniversaire—Janvier 1897

LE NOIR roc courroucé que la bise le roule
Ne s'arrêtera ni sous de pieuses mains
Tâtant sa ressemblance avec les maux humains
Comme pour en bénir quelque funeste moule.

Ici presque toujours si le ramier roucoule
Cet immatériel deuil opprime de maints
Nubiles plis l'astre mûri des lendemains
Dont un scintillement argentera la foule.

Qui cherche, parcourant le solitaire bond
Tantôt extérieur de notre vagabond—
Verlaine? Il est caché parmi l'herbe, Verlaine

A ne surprendre que naïvement d'accord
La lèvre sans y boire ou tarir son haleine
Un peu profond ruisseau calomnié la mort.

TOMBEAU

Anniversaire—Janvier 1897

THE black rock angered that the northern blast
rolls it will not be stopped by pious hands
testing if for all human ills it stands
to bless some fatal mold where it was cast.

Usually if the ringdove coos here
this immaterial grief with many a cloud
enfolding crushes tomorrow's ripened star
whose scintillations will besilver the crowd.

Who, following the solitary bound
just now external of our vagabond—
who seeks Verlaine? He is hidden in the grass,

Verlaine but to surprise naïvely at peace
the lips without drinking there or stopping his breath
a shallow stream calumniated Death.

HOMMAGE

Le silence déjà funèbre d'une moire
Dispose plus qu'un pli seul sur le mobilier
Que doit un tassement du principal pilier
Précipiter avec le manque de mémoire.

Notre si vieil ébat triomphal du grimoire,
Hiéroglyphes dont s'exalte le millier
A propager de l'aile un frisson familier!
Enfouissez-le-moi plutôt dans une armoire.

Du souriant fracas originel haï
Entre elles de clartés maîtresses a jailli
Jusque vers un parvis né pour leur simulacre,

Trompettes tout haut d'or pâmé sur les vélins,
Le dieu Richard Wagner irradiant un sacre
Mal tu par l'encre même en sanglots sibyllins.

HOMMAGE

THE SILENCE already funereal of a moire
arranges more than one fold on the table
which when none remembers any more
a sinking of the main leg will let crumble.

Our so old conquering zest of conjuring,
hieroglyphics giving the thousands an ecstasy
to propagate the familiar thrill of a wing!
Stick all that in an old clothespress for me.

From the smiling fracas original and hated
(very loud trumpets of gold that swooned
    on the vellums)
among those of masterly clarities has gushed

as far as the parvis born for their simulacrum,
the god Richard Wagner radiant, self-consecrated,
by ink in sibylline sobs but badly hushed.

AU SEUL SOUCI...

Au seul souci de voyager
Outre une Inde splendide et trouble
—Ce salut soit le messager
Du temps, cap que ta poupe double

Comme sur quelque vergue bas
Plongeante avec la caravelle
Ecumait toujours en ébats
Un oiseau d'annonce nouvelle

Qui criait monotonement
Sans que la barre ne varie
Un inutile gisement
Nuit, désespoir et pierrerie

Par son chant reflété jusqu'au
Sourire du pâle Vasco.

AU SEUL SOUCI...

To THE sole concern for the passage
past an India splendid and troubled
—may this greeting be the message
of time, cape your poop doubles

as on some yard low-riding
plunging with the ship
foamed ever in playful dips
a bird of recent tidings

which cried in monotone
without the tiller's veering
a futile coastal-bearing:
Night, despair, precious stones

by its song reflected just to
the smile of pallid Vasco.

TOUTE L'ÂME RÉSUMÉE...

TOUTE l'âme résumée
Quand lente nous l'expirons
Dans plusieurs ronds de fumée
Abolis en autres ronds

Atteste quelque cigare
Brûlant savamment pour peu
Que la cendre se sépare
De son clair baiser de feu

Ainsi le chœur des romances
A la lèvre vole-t-il
Exclus-en si tu commences
Le réel parce que vil

Le sens trop précis rature
Ta vague littérature

TOUTE L'ÂME RÉSUMÉE...

ALL the soul summarized
when slowly we exhale
smoke-rings that arise
and other rings annul

attests some cigar
burning shrewdly if
all the ash drop off
its clear kiss of fire

Thus the singing choir
does it fly to your lips?
Exclude if you begin
the real which is cheap

its too sharp sense rubs thin
your vague literature

AUTRES POËMES ET SONNETS

I

Tout Orgueil fume-t-il du soir,
Torche dans un branle étouffée
Sans que l'immortelle bouffée
Ne puisse à l'abandon surseoir!

La chambre ancienne de l'hoir
De maint riche mais chu trophée
Ne serait pas même chauffée
S'il survenait par le couloir.

Affres du passé nécessaires
Agrippant comme avec des serres
Le sépulcre de désaveu,

Sous un marbre lourd qu'elle isole
Ne s'allume pas d'autre feu
Que la fulgurante console.

II

Surgi de la croupe et du bond
D'une verrerie éphémère
Sans fleurir la veillée amère
Le col ignoré s'interrompt.

Je crois bien que deux bouches n'ont
Bu, ni son amant ni ma mère,
Jamais à la même Chimère,
Moi, sylphe de ce froid plafond!

AUTRES POËMES ET SONNETS

I

DOES all Pride smoke out night,
torch by shaking snuffed
without the immortal puff
being able to keep alight?

The ancient bedroom of the heir
with many a rich fallen trophy
wouldn't even be warmed if he
came in from the corridor.

Anguishes doomed by the past
as with claws clutching fast
denial's sepulcher,

under a heavy marble,
isolated, is lighted no fire
save the glittering console table.

II

Sprung from the leap and the croup
of a glassware ephemeral
flowering no bitter vigil
the neck forgotten stops.

Sylph of this cold ceiling, I
well believe two mouths never,
neither mother nor her lover,
drank the same phantasy!

Le pur vase d'aucun breuvage
Que l'inexhàustible veuvage
Agonise mais ne consent,

Naïf baiser des plus funèbres!
A rien expirer annonçant
Une rose dans les ténèbres.

III

Une dentelle s'abolit
Dans le doute du Jeu suprême
A n'entr'ouvrir comme un blasphème
Qu'absence éternelle de lit.

Cet unanime blanc conflit
D'une guirlande avec la même,
Enfui contre la vitre blême
Flotte plus qu'il n'ensevelit.

Mais, chez qui du rêve se dore
Tristement dort une mandore
Au creux néant musicien

Telle que vers quelque fenêtre
Selon nul ventre que le sien,
Filial on aurait pu naître.

The vase pure of any potion
save the widowhood unspent
dies but does not consent,

naïve kiss of the most dour!
to breathe an annunciation
of a rose in the obscure.

III

Abolished the curtains half-spread
of the supreme Game in doubt
(like a blasphemy) reveal but
eternal absence of bed.

This unanimous white clash
of a garland with its twin
escaped against the pale glass
floats more than buries in.

But with him of the gilded dream
a mandola sleeps in sorrow
in a hollow of musical zero

such that toward some pane
involving no womb but its own
one might be born as son.

QUELLE SOIE...

QUELLE soie aux baumes de temps
Où la Chimère s'exténue
Vaut la torse et native nue
Que, hors de ton miroir, tu tends!

Les trous de drapeaux méditants
S'exaltent dans notre avenue:
Moi, j'ai ta chevelure nue
Pour enfouir mes yeux contents.

Non! La bouche ne sera sûre
De rien goûter à sa morsure,
S'il ne fait, ton princier amant,

Dans la considérable touffe
Expirer, comme un diamant,
Le cri des Gloires qu'il étouffe.

QUELLE SOIE...

WHAT silk that time has steeped in balm
upon which died the tired Chimera
is worth the native cloud you comb
of twisted hair before your mirror?

The holes of thoughtful flags out there
along our street are raised in pride:
but I, I have your naked hair
wherein my happy eyes can hide.

No! the mouth will not be sure
in its bite of finding savor,
unless he, your princely lover,

breathe out, diamond-like, in your
considerable tuft the cry
of Glories stifled as they die.

M'INTRODUIRE...

M'INTRODUIRE dans ton histoire
C'est en héros effarouché
S'il a du talon nu touché
Quelque gazon de territoire

A des glaciers attentatoire
Je ne sais le naïf péché
Que tu n'auras pas empêché
De rire très haut sa victoire

Dis si je ne suis pas joyeux
Tonnerre et rubis aux moyeux
De voir en l'air que ce feu troue

Avec des royaumes épars
Comme mourir pourpre la roue
Du seul vespéral de mes chars.

M'INTRODUIRE...

To BRING myself into your tale
is as a hero much afraid
if he has touched with naked heel
any grass-plot of that glade

Ravisher of glaciers I
know no artless sin that after
hindering you'll not deny
its very loud victorious laughter

And am I not joyous, say,
thunder and rubies to the naves
to see in the air pierced by fire

among realms scattered and afar
as in a crimson death the wheel
of my chariots' only vesperal.

A LA NUE...

A LA nue accablante tu
Basse de basalte et de laves
A même les échos esclaves
Par une trompe sans vertu

Quel sépulcral naufrage (tu
Le sais, écume, mais y baves)
Suprême une entre les épaves
Abolit le mât dévêtu

Ou cela que furibond faute
De quelque perdition haute
Tout l'abîme vain éployé

Dans le si blanc cheveu qui traîne
Avarement aura noyé
Le flanc enfant d'une sirène.

A LA NUE...

Stilled by the crushing cloud
low of basalt and lava
by even the enslaved
echoes of a trumpet not loud

what sepulchral shipwreck
(you know, foam, though you slobber)
supreme among derelicts
knocked the stripped mast over

or that which furious failing
of some high perdition
(all the vain abyss spread wide)

in the so white hair trailing
will have drowned miser-fashion
some siren's infant side.

MES BOUQUINS...

Mes bouquins refermés sur le nom de Paphos,
Il m'amuse d'élire avec le seul génie
Une ruine, par mille écumes bénie
Sous l'hyacinthe, au loin, de ses jours triomphaux.

Coure le froid avec ses silences de faux,
Je n'y hululerai pas de vide nénie
Si ce très blanc ébat au ras du sol dénie
A tout site l'honneur du paysage faux.

Ma faim qui d'aucuns fruits ici ne se régale
Trouve en leur docte manque une saveur égale:
Qu'un éclate de chair humain et parfumant!

Le pied sur quelque givre où notre amour tisonne,
Je pense plus longtemps peut-être éperdument
A l'autre, au sein brûlé d'une antique amazone.

MES BOUQUINS...

My old books closed on Paphos' name, I elect
at the whim of the one genius, far away,
a ruin, blessed by a thousand foamy flecks
under hyacinth, in its triumphal days.

Let the cold run with its silences of scythes,
I shall not ululate here an empty wail
if this very white frolic skimming the ground denies
to any landscape the honor of being unreal.

My hunger that will feast on no fruits here
finds in their learned lack an equal taste:
although this fragrant human flesh should burst!

Feet on some wyvern where our love stirs the fire,
longer perhaps distracted I brood on
the other, with seared breast of an ancient Amazon.

NOTES

In these notes I have attempted to include the interpretations of the various poems by critics who have commented on them. Sometimes my own point of view took issue with them, but it, like theirs, is merely one man's opinion. What I have written was the particular impression I got of this Old Man of the Sea as I wrestled with him—and lost.

I

Salut   page 2

On a first reading this opening poem will mean little to the reader. The occasion for which it was written may somewhat apologize for and clarify the obviously intended feeling of obfuscation he wanted to give. As toastmaster for a banquet, given by the review *La Plume,* in 1893, Mallarmé, the acknowledged *maître* of the younger writers, rises to his feet and clears his throat, in which already death had announced its intentions by making the voice sound husky. Delicately, almost diffidently, this little gray man lifts a glass of champagne in one hand and deftly produces—with somewhat of a magician's air as he fetches forth the rabbit from the silk hat—the manuscript of the sonnet that had finally satisfied him, after Lord knows how many hours of refining and condensing. His method was always that of the silversmith who arranges elaborately yards of fine wire, solders them into an inch-small butterfly, and says, "Voilà!" The effort is no longer apparent: the work of art remains, a unified, organic thing. He immediately admits that it is "Nothing," and thereby disarms potential opponents. The virgin verse and the foam on the wine are of equal value, delightful and evanescent. In the half-light of the banquet room the pale liquid in the glass may well have seemed almost invisible. Only a few bubbles indicate ephemerally the limits of the container. The play of gleams and shadows makes him think of supernatural aqueous creatures, suddenly reduced in size, and he pretends to see a group of sirens bathing and diving; nor could his Gallic mind resist the temptation of pointing out the pulchritude of these callipygic young women. (This preoccupation with the nude is characteristic of much of his verse.) Now, on this ocean conjured by his imagination, as captain of the vessel embarked on the perilous voyage of a literary life, he speaks from the poop to the young sailors, his disciples, who *are,* he says, the prow of his ship and are narrowly aware of the chill thunder crashing around the bold cutwater. Admitting himself to be a bit high (for I refuse to accept, as a translation of "une ivresse belle," "frenzy sublime" by Arthur Ellis, "a fine ebriety" by Roger Fry, or "a beautiful intoxication" by Grange Woolley), he humorously protests that he can stand upright holding his glass, like the tulip that suggested to Hafiz the figure of the steadfast tippler. With no fear of the pitching deck—i.e., the floor which may already have seemed to be revolving gently—he names "Solitude, star, rock-coast," all of which are the sailor's background and destiny, and proposes his toast to whatever it may be that is worth the chiseling and polishing, the night vigils and soul sweat, the loneliness and lack of appreciation that go into the making of poetry, "the white concern of our sail." It is also characteristic that he willfully switches the adjective. Nor does he speciously promise a safe harbor after the voyage. Thibaudet, p. 311, is to be envied for two fine phrases: "In this fragile glass from Murano, the poetic play launches, with all sails spread, a Bucentaur of poets," and, concerning the final stanza: "the splendid sheaf of the last tercet! Not a phrase, but a constellation of fifteen words, with the white page around it." More factually, the German, Wais, p. 395, records that the banquet was the first occasion since the days of Racine that—in the words of Achille Delaroche—the poet was revealed as a master. He also mentions that the white, blank paper appears in other poems by the toastmaster and that the sirens evoke the Argonaut saga in which Orpheus, the first poet, made the musical bird-women drown themselves in jealousy of his superior music.

Placet futile   page 4

A charming little rococo piece, quite in the mood, if not in the style, of Verlaine's *Fêtes galantes.* It is playful, precious, and as delicately made as the dishes displayed at the Sèvres factory, just outside of Paris. The abbé, the confection, the rouge, and the lapdog were stage properties of the eighteenth-century school of art, and not one is missing. Therefore I deferentially refuse to subscribe to the astonishing remark of Thibaudet, p. 74: "This charming affectation recalls, rather than the eighteenth century, the *Adonis,* or the poets of the age of Elizabeth, and most, Gongora." The raspberry-colored lips and sheep-white teeth of the royal laughter fit excellently into this sort of salon *objet d'art.* The Cupid, who bears fans as wings, is as roseately rotund as those Loves who hover ready to waft the barque of ladies and gallants in Watteau's "L'Embarquement pour Cythère." In an earlier version of the poem the heroine was merely a duchess. The lines essentially different run: "I have long dreamed of being, O duchess, the Hebe who laughs on your cup . . . but I am a poet, a lesser thing than an abbé . . . appoint me . . . and Boucher will paint me fluting with sleeping hands," etc. Wais, p. 341, complains about the auxiliary verbs and the adverbs; elsewhere he laments, p. 347, the poet's use of " 'seltenen' und krausen" words, like *poind* and *pastille.* He also, p. 33, mistakes "framboise" for "Erdbeeren," a grave difference. But here we are, wrapping up this delicate bit of porcelain in scholarly tissue paper. Let's see what he does say. He kneels in silken breeches before the princess whose raspberry-hued lips are just about to touch the cup above the Hebe, while the lambs imagined from her white teeth are frisking to minuets, played as by Couperin or Rameau, or a peruked orchestra under the discreet chestnut trees of Versailles.

Une négresse par le démon secouée   page 6

To temper a too hasty decision against this poem, the reader might remind himself of the lines from Catullus, XVI: "nam castum esse decet pium poetam / ipsum versiculos nihil necesse est"; or of Martial's (X, 1, 4): "Lasciva est nobis pagina, vita proba," translated by Mainard as "Si ma plume est une putain, / Ma vie est une sainte"; or the injunction on the Garter of the English order. The poet, at twenty, wanted to shock his readers, as did Baudelaire with his "Une charogne." The French have always been a tolerant people, especially to literary sins, which are by no means to be confused with sins against literature. The poem first appeared in a two-volume anthology, *Le Parnasse satyrique du XIXe siècle,* published by Poulet-Malassis, Bruxelles, 1863–1866, decorated by Félicien Rops. The poem was not reprinted by Edmond Deman, in *Les Poésies de Stéphane Mallarmé*, Bruxelles, 1899, but the two editions I am using include it. At least, the poet erred in excellent company. The figures of the gazelle and shell are apropos. For the latter, I refer you to the note on Verlaine's "Coquillages," in my translations from that poet. The shell Mallarmé was thinking of was the *Cypraea mus*. The astute Norman Douglas, in his collection of limericks, has a note that explains the last stanza.

Les Fenêtres   page 8

The pessimism expressed in this piece by a young man of twenty-four follows the recipe philosophical and the style of Baudelaire. Many astute young people today feel, too, that life is a hospital. It is another youthful delusion when he feels himself bored, prematurely aged, ready for death, even by suicide. Mallarmé was professedly not a Christian, so the holy oils were naturally annoying. There have been French poets who, after some rebellious sacrilegious poems in youth, repented and slid into heaven at the last minute; but he was not one of them. His pessimism was no doubt increased by the death of his sister, Marie, when the unarmored dreamer was only seventeen; and a young American, Harriet, who probably brought the poetry of Poe to his attention, died in the same year. His sensitive nature undoubtedly got a great shock that shook his faith. The present poem is entirely symbolic. A sick man drags himself to the window, yearning for sunlight. The curtain is really the veil between the two worlds, and he yearns for the eternal verities beyond the banal. The wall that shuts him in is a cross, the ultimate of tired suffering. In his stanza on the galleys we find the first real poetry thus far. But this lovely vision is merely a temporary relief. He decides on flight. This was precisely Faust's problem, in his soliloquy, lines 640–651, and "lavé d'éternelles rosées" was borrowed from "in deinem Thau gesund mich baden," as "Au ciel antérieur où fleurit la Beauté" anticipates "Pulchérie" from the "Prose" of twenty years later, and she seems to be the apotheosis of the Marie-Harriet symbol of childhood's lost happiness. There is much of Hamlet's soliloquy here, as of Faust's.

Angoisse   page 12

This, quite naturally, is almost an anthology piece because it seems at first reading to belong to the ever-popular bedroom type. Here we find Mallarmé's youthful *Nachtbewusstsein*. He has got his nose out of that ditch he dug in the spring earth and he is with a woman. The sonnet was originally entitled "A une putain," and would have been more ironical than the present one. Let us not condemn the young fellow for wanting to have a look around town and a good night's sleep. Yet Thibaudet hastens to assure one, p. 33, that "ce tourment, chez Mallarmé, est un tourment littéraire autant qu'un tourment humain," and Wais, p. 52, writes: "Zum

Pfühl der Dirne ging er zweifellos rein *literarisch,* bewegt durch die sehr authentischen, hundertfach nachgeahmten Apostrophen Baudelaires an der Buhlerin, die auf Banville oder Cazalis ähnlich wirkten." I am relieved to learn this, but the resulting poems, in no case, come up to the beauty of "Mère des souvenirs, maîtresse des maîtresses!" The lofty Saint John of the Cross was able to make use of what may have been a more tender experience, with telling effect, in "The Obscure Night of the Soul":

> O night more lovely than the dawn of light,
> O night that broughtest us,
> Lover to love's sight,
> Lover with loved in marriage of delight.

> (Translation by Arthur Symons)

Sappho and Catullus expressed immemorably their joys and sorrows of love; Musset whined over his grisettes; Byron bragged about his women, from bakers' wives to duchesses; Goethe flurried the hearts of all the parsons' daughters to work himself up to making a poem; Swinburne flung his youthful handful of "red roses in the face of the nun," i.e., Victorian England (T. Hardy); Dowson got off one immortal poem to a barmaid—but poor little Mallarmé, whose wife was several years his senior and whom he had married after a trial voyage to England, hopes for nothing save a brief respite from loneliness and a gentle hangover of remorse. But the woman, she is the eternal prototype of those blowsy hard-faced wenches who are to be seen better in Paris than in most other great cities. Is she not La Goulue, or Daudet's Sapho, or that splendidly depraved little Norman, Virginie, with the obscene Medusan hair, whose bizarre and lubricious English used to amuse the evening strolls of the last expatriates in Montparnasse in the summer of 1939, and whose daughter was there to take over when we returned in 1948? "Rideaux," line 6, comes from Baudelaire's "Une martyre," stanza 9.

118

And one is thankful to know that the poet's sterility was but a passing affair, for his wife gave him two children.

Tristesse d'été page 14

Thibaudet, p. 240, charges our poet with imitating rhymes from his master, the same ones that had "falsified" the *Fleurs du Mal*. It took me some time to discover these rhymes in "Lesbos," stanza 4, and in "Chanson d'après-midi," stanza 6. They don't seem so bad to me, as used here, for the summer mood of the sleepy couple that had been making love, apparently on a sandy beach that makes the otherwise dull Mme Mallarmé suddenly remember the mummies she had seen in the recently acquired Egyptian collection in the Louvre, and prattle about them. Wais analyzes this mediocre butterfly of a poem into tatters. He finds in the woman "a dangerous opponent," but it strikes me that he is remembering his Schopenhauer and Nietzsche. I just refuse to think that Mallarmé's wife had such a speech in her, for she told Mme de Banville that she never understood her husband's poetry. Again, as in "Angoisse," he discovers the "Néant" in the woman's hair. He is always frolicking about in hair. He must have acquired some childish fixation on it. Maybe his mother or his sister had a *belle chevelure*. He had a fine crop himself; but why must he drag it into almost all the poems to Méry Laurent later? One remembers here the definite stand that Porphyria's lover took on the matter: he merely up and strangled her with it. Aristotle in his physiology book has a section on the virtues of sleep after just this sort of "lutte."

Aumône page 16

This terza rima form is past my ingenuity, so the poem is presented with only the first and third lines rhyming, or almost. I have never yet seen a good translation of a Petrarchan sonnet, because no one can handle four rhymes without violating the original. Thibaudet is reticent about this poem, except for noting the ironic final line. On the other hand, Wais, pp. 48 ff., has a fine time making himself an explication in which he remembers beggars scattered through literature, even the one in Molière's *Don Juan* who appears in Baudelaire's swan song for the hero. The origin of the piece is attributed to the bankrupt philanthropy that disenchanted the finer spirits after the fiasco of 1848. As usual, the poet deliberately mixes up his syntax, a trick the reader will resent increasingly as we proceed. Most attempts at a critique of Mallarmé's work are as fuddling as the versions of the seven blind men who "saw" the elephant! The poet has had a profound effect on poetry since his time, but it is impossible to believe that people in 1998, the anniversary of his death, will spend much time in unraveling his abracadabras. The advice of the donor here to the beggar seems, briefly, to be as follows: Listen, brother, don't feel that you must do anything practical with this money. I'm not a preacher. Take it and squander it in some "splendid bizarre sin," something you couldn't otherwise do. Go to a café, that poor man's church whose incense is tobacco smoke, get drunk, fill your throat with hot stars, then stroll along and look at the rich men in their gilded pleasure-domes. Buy yourself a new feather for your old hat, that's as good as a candle for some saint you don't cease to believe in. But, above all, don't buy any bread. Just take it and waste it, and forget me.

Hérodiade   page 20

I must summarize from Thibaudet, pp. 387–392, the most pertinent remarks. In *Divagations,* Mallarmé announced a prelude and a finale. The fragment as we have it is probably one of the few of his works that have had any effect on poetry and any circulation among readers. Written after "L'Après-midi d'un Faune," his greatest single piece of work in what we may call the "Symbolist" style, he chose to put it before that in his book. It marks the culmination of his Parnassianistic period, the influence of Gautier, Baudelaire, and Banville, and thus becomes "a stairway of gold uniting a Parnassian desert and a lush land of Symbolism. The brilliance of its coloring is worked into a Byzantine mosaic of cold stones."

In proof of these statements, here I must give a few excerpts from other writers who influenced the poem.

From Baudelaire: "La Beauté":

> Je suis belle, ô mortels! comme un rêve de pierre . . .

> Je trône dans l'azur comme un sphinx incompris;
> J'unis un cœur de neige à la blancheur des cygnes; . . .
> Et jamais je ne pleure et jamais je ne ris.

> Car j'ai, pour fasciner ces dociles amants,
> De purs miroirs qui font toutes choses plus belles:
> Mes yeux, mes larges yeux aux clartés éternelles!

From "Avec ses vêtements":

> Comme le sable morne et l'azur des déserts,
> Insensibles tous deux à l'humaine souffrance . . .

Is this not quite in the key of Herodias when she says:

> Je veux que mes cheveux qui ne sont pas des fleurs
> A répandre l'oubli des humaines douleurs . . . ?

And here are the words: *serpents, indifférence, inviolé, or, diamants* of Mallarmé's princess, who might have said the final lines from Baudelaire's

> . . . comme un astre inutile,
> La froide majesté de la femme stérile.

From Flaubert's *Trois Contes,* here follow a few selections from "Hérodias." "A light purple gown enveloped her to the sandals. Having hurriedly left her room, she was without necklaces and earrings; a black tress of hair fell over one arm, and the end of it curled in the valley between her breasts. Her nostrils, greatly curved, were trembling; the joy of victory lighted her body, and in a strong voice which shook the Tetrarch, she said . . . " A page or so later: "She had aged the Tetrarch." There is a little quarrel and she retorts: "I got a fine maintenance on entering your family!" Presently we meet her more famous daughter, who was "just as Herodias used to be in her youth." I beg to be excused from getting started on that dance! In *Salammbô,* 1862, the princess is presented as devoted to a claustral life which had been established by a cult worshiping the moon-goddess. Her clothes, however, have always the same metallic richness as those of the other royal exotic girls who wander coldly, proudly, and futilely through the pages of the Parnassians. In her final appearance, she has her feet on an ivory stool, and her arms are heavily braceleted. She wears a dress imitating the scales of a fish, shining as with nacre, and her breasts are chummily visible through two moon-shaped slashes in the material, while the nipples are hidden by carbuncle pendants. Her hair is dressed with peacock's feathers and jewels, and she sits in a hieratic attitude.

All these women are cut from one and the same stuff, and certain it is that the daughters of Herodias haunted the visions of many artists during the rest of the century. Gustave Moreau painted "Salomé" in 1876, and another version, either before or after. Huysmans in *A Rebours,* 1884, described the pictures and helped found an artistic cult. Oscar Wilde and Richard Strauss were aware of all these sources. So was Max Klinger when he made the polychrome statue of a similar heroine in Leipsic, the "Judith." The present specimen is as convincing as any of the lot. Let us see what the critics have to say of her.

A. R. Chisholm's three books, concise and stimulating as they are, should be read by all beginners with Mallarmé. Literary sources are indicated, and the philosophic background of the century, in its relation to Symbolism, is presented adequately. One does not need to involve himself with all the categories suggested, such as angelism, occultism, etc. Slighter studies by Leconte de Lisle, Rimbaud, Heredia, and a grand finale by Valéry cast light on the literary evolution of the period. Since the author writes in English, there is no point in my making excerpts.

Wais provides a few usable notes: Mallarmé in 1898 wrote to his publisher that he had finished the triptych, but Dr. Bonniot did not allow the first section to be published until late 1926. (Poets' daughters ought not marry into the *petite bourgeoisie*.) Wais discovers that, philosophically, the poem represents the fall of an unreal abstract aesthetic idealism; from a literary analysis, there emerges the unmasking of a bodiless unfeeling ideal of beauty, according to the Parnassians, the last traces of which appear in Whistler's *Ten o'Clock*; and the fragment portrays, he alleges (p. 111), "daemonically proud girls who suffer from a biological glow which they believe they have overcome, yet it comes creeping back again and avenges itself!" Yes, she is the sister of Hippolytus. There is only one thing to be done with such girls, but it seems not to have happened in the poem as it now stands.

Everyone who has written on the piece is reminded of analogous literary characters: Diana, Narcissus, the Sphinx, La Joconda, et cetera. And I must have a word about the tower dwellers in the past. The first one I know is the princess from 3,000 B.C., presented in Maspero's *Les Contes populaires de l'Egypte ancienne,* whose father shut her up so she couldn't get married. But there was finally, thank goodness, a prince who learned to fly. He got there. I suppose Simeon Stylites was a later example. I recently saw again Bishop Hatto's tower in Bingen on the Rhine. The grotesque Quasimodo lived his life high up in Notre-Dame. And that poor doomed Lady of Shalott! May she conclude the brood. So, Herodias, in the "overture ancienne," lives with her old nurse, in a tower in Idumaea. Mallarmé cleverly does not allow her to be seen, thus whetting one's appetite. The Nurse soliloquizes, rather elegantly, too, for a woman of her humble station, at dawn. The tower is filled with glittering war trophies from family conquests. These seem to constitute almost the only furniture, but in a desert country one can get along with very little, it seems. The vaults below hold the urns of the ashes of the dead former kings. It is like a mausoleum. Outside is a pool so dead that it frightens away the very birds. The sensible Nurse sees in her ward's renunciation of life a violation against nature, and she quite frankly says so. She describes the empty bed, the tapestries, the fading flowers in the room. She hears a voice like an incantation, calling up the vanished glories of the line: "a voice arises as if a lacy cloth that had long since been laid over a pile of monstrances and censers were letting the old veiled brilliance mount through its meshes." It fades away, and the sight of the dead pool recalls the barren reality of the present. A clepsydra monotonously drips out the hours while the Princess walks alone in the chill of morning, when even the flowers (like her own virgin bloom) are shivering, and at nightfall, when the pomegranates are nipped (a cleft pomegranate is the emblem of a broken heart). The king, her father (who has certainly no resemblance to the Biblical Antipas), is off in the Alps among fierce glaciers which reflect the gleams of his armor. Will he return in time to save this wayward girl from herself? Then a ray of dawn enters the window, and the image of a dead star is visible. It is an ominous ending.

"Scène" opens rather illogically, with the girl in bed. Her chilly nature makes itself immediately apparent when she rebukes her nurse—who must in the past have performed even more intimate services—for wanting to straighten her up and comb her hair. This *noli me tangere* attitude gives any male reader a profound inexact pain. Then the girl brags about her power over the lions—presumably, this symbolically represents her control over the fleshly lusts of the world—and then she undresses, in a very pleasant strip tease, before the pool in the famous mirror scene. She doesn't want her hair combed or perfumed. She just wants to preserve that virginal sterile metallic appearance, like a New York mannequin, or a new porcelain bed pan. Throughout the scene she is so aloof and affected that one wants to spank her. But she has had doubts of her dreams as she gazed in the mirror pool. She is, as we would say nowadays, trying to analyze herself. The Nurse is the same aged pandress as Juliet's. She had a good time in her youth and naturally wants her charge to enjoy herself. Yet the pure egoism of the princess holds her back. She is too proud to please anyone but herself. She is Penthesilea of the Amazons, all over again. So she goes on, in this self-delusion, dreaming of mines of jewels as fabulous as those of King Solomon—and as nonexistent. Mallarmé does make beautiful images, what with a catalogue of jewels, perfumes, but these perfect and glittering sections are merely stuck on to the poem. They are on it rather than in it. The poem ends with the princess still not knowing what she wants. But in the interim between this conclusion and the next poem, one must remember the Biblical story. She must have wanted the Baptist. And, by virtue of his future sainthood, he was bound to scorn her. All this goes on behind scenes.

Then we come to the "Cantique de saint Jean." This is one of the most condensed poems in the book. Every line is full, as a small bud implicitly contains a large flower or leaf. Once unfolded, these tight lines reveal much the same scene as the painting by Puvis de Chavannes in the Panthéon. Only here the head has been severed from the neck as it speaks—after the first, introductory, stanza. Mauron (Fry, p. 100) mentions the coincidence of St. John's Day and the summer solstice. The sun at its farthest north seems to halt before it returns southward. Similarly, the head at the top of its arc. The head has felt the final shudder as spirit was severed from flesh, and has now, for the supreme moment, a view all round. Here is the realm of absolute zero, the surpasser of glaciers! The *faux* is both symbolic, Death's well-known scythe, and specific, the headsman's sword, a *falx,* in Roman antiquity a weapon like the falchion. The combination of glowing sunlight and blood is effective as visual imagery. The head, in its uttermost flight, feels its beatification assured, because its martyrdom seems to have been predestined by the unquestionable wisdom of God. One never quite understands this poem, nor does he ever forget it. It has the power of all mysteries: it occasions always a faint scratching in the brain by the unsolvable questions posed. The packed and choppy lines are slight help to the translator, and the absent punctuation was a vexation of spirit. I should like to read a period after the first and fourth stanzas. Mauron (Fry, p. 101) says he would like a period after stanza 4.

L'Après-midi d'un Faune   page 46

This poem is as shy as a young deer, and only several readings will gain its confidence—unless it be that the music of Debussy will also help, for he has understood the poem better than the critics do. Herodias is cold and aloof; the Faun is evasive and speaks, so to say, from "l'horizon de ses roseaux." Both are to be conquered slowly, and the earlier victory will be through visualizing and feeling in the fingers the richness and sensuous qualities of the proud princess. The highest pleasures one can get from the "Faun" will be the musical quality of the words themselves, in their seemingly careless but so artful and willful disarrangement from syntax, and the intolerance of the common decent rules of coherence. I object to the almost universal fallacy that French is a musical language. There are a dozen others that far surpass it for sheer euphony, Italian and Spanish, to mention the best known. The accursed eternal nasals must not be sounded too resonantly and the poem were better read in whispers or murmurs, as dreams speak. And the poem is, above all, a dream phantasy. The difference between the effects of the two so-called "masterpieces" is precisely that between Parnassianism and Symbolism: the eye versus the ear.

Rather perversely, let me begin the symposium from the critics negatively. George Moore, *Confessions,* p. 58: "There were for contrast Mallarmé's Tuesday evenings, a few friends

126

sitting around the hearth, the lamp on the table. I have met none whose conversation was so fruitful, but with the exception of his early verses I cannot say I ever frankly enjoyed his poetry. When I knew him he had just published the celebrated 'L'Après-midi d'un Faune': the first poem written in accordance with the theory of Symbolism . . . I thought it absurdly obscure. But what is symbolism? Vulgarly speaking, saying the opposite to what you mean. For example [Moore is speaking, here, of the "Hommage" to Wagner], you want to say that music, which is the new art, is replacing the old art, which is poetry. First symbol: a house in which there is a funeral, the pall extends over the furniture. The house is poetry, poetry is dead. Second symbol: 'notre vieux grimoire,' *grimoire* is the parchment, parchment is used for writing, therefore, *grimoire* is the symbol for literature, 'd'où s'exaltent les milliers,' thousands of what? of letters of course. We have heard a great deal in England of Browning's obscurity. The 'Red Cotton Nightcap Country' is child's play compared to a sonnet by a determined symbolist such as Mallarmé . . ." (It is only fair to add that Mr. Moore later in his book, pp. 190–194, expresses himself rather more favorably toward the poet and translates two of the prose poems, a trick almost anyone could have fetched off.)

Symbolism has always been so much an agent for the transmission of thought that it is a bit difficult for me to understand why the English and French, just at the turn of the century, found the new poetry so abstruse. I have omitted the Americans, because only Vielé-Griffin, Stuart Merrill, Whistler, and Henry James had ever heard of Mallarmé at that time, and they all lived abroad. We grow up with symbolism as with our mothers' milk. Symbols are displayed on our monies, in the churches, in the gestures we use in lieu of speech; even our facial expressions are symbols representing a state of feeling. In the myths of various countries, in the morality plays, the legends, say, of Don Juan, Siegfried, Beowulf, Roland, Faust, and in all the trappings of heraldry we are usually aware of the emotional, mental, or moral element for which they stand. We speak of the scales of Justice, our duty to the Flag, the pipe of peace, the olive branch, the eye of God or the law, et cetera. These are merely signs for the thing signified, a visual and poetic way of naming something otherwise abstract. As Goethe says: "Alles Vergängliche / Ist nur ein Gleichnis." Once adapted, a symbol soon becomes trite, but that has never interfered with its circulation, just as one takes a thin dime as readily as a mint-new coin. It is only with new, and often arbitrary, symbols that difficulty is encountered. Therefore, Plato uses allegories and the New Testament the parables. New ideas are explained in old symbols, e.g., the mustardseed of faith, the mountain of doubt. One remembers that because he can see the symbols themselves. Thus, the last sonnets of Mallarmé interest me far more than his juvenile lamentations and wistful bellyaches. These nauseate; the later ones tantalize, irritating until finally understanding bursts through their apparent difficulties. Like crusty mature oysters, they may contain the rarest pearls. Mallarmé uses the ship as a symbol for literature, the mirror for narcissism, the sterile Herodias for the decline of culture in modern civilization, the Faun for the unattainable dreamed desires. A woman's golden hair is the sunset, her white milk the essence of womanhood itself, the mandola the hollow musical womb from which the poet is engendered. Et cetera. Despite the symbol of the Faun, as man's dream-desires, he is as alive and vigorous as the little satyr playing with the nanny goat in *il cabineto segreto* at the Museum of Naples, devoted to the erotica discovered in the ruins of Pompeii and Herculaneum.

The following is a précis from Thibaudet, pp. 393-402. "The poem is a morsel for connoisseurs; but even in its freshness one finds evidences of the growing obscurity, 'spaces of silence around the symbols,' and of all that gives the later verse its mystery and elusiveness. It is an amusing and sensual eclogue which leads us to symbolic and metaphysical latencies. . . .

In its abundance of lilies and stars it recalls Banville and Mendès, but its immediate motif was probably suggested by a painting by Boucher in the Louvre." (This might have been Correggio's "Jupiter and Antiope," or somebody's "Pan and Syrinx." There are so many of these ungentlemanly gods!) Thibaudet proceeds:—but I shall select parts loosely, so there's no use punctuating with quotation marks. He finds something of the influence of Praxiteles in the little flower-wound horns, and the ears remind him of the poet's own! The evening wood is golden and festive. Aetna, like a burning heart, is visited by Venus. In the course of his amatory divagations the Faun dreams of nymphs, Syrinx, and the goddess herself. Of course, there had been a small renaissance of such art in the Louvre, which gave Verlaine his *Fêtes galantes*.

Here in the lush setting, near a swamp, man's primitive desire is wide awake. He feels that he must possess one of these naked bathers, and failing that, he picks up a couple of nymphs, in each other's "perilous arms." When they too escape him, he contents himself with blowing bubbles from grapeskins, a symbol of intoxication. Then he falls asleep.

Wais, pp. 150–159, contributes the following: In 1865 Mallarmé stopped work on the "Hérodias," and Banville suggested that he try a monologue for Coquelin senior. So an early version of the "Faun" was finished and presented at the Odéon, with slight success. Eleven years later a second version was published: the first mature work of the author, a poem stripped of the influence of Baudelaire. Shortly afterward a limited edition with decorations by Manet appeared. (This was probably the one treasured by Huysmans's des Esseintes.) Baudelaire, in his prose poem "Le Fou et la Vénus," is sympathetic toward the fool; but Mallarmé is inexorable to his Faun who throws away the flute (of art?) in his erotic contemplation of the cleanly nymphs.

This poem has had more influence and has received wider circulation than any other in the book. Bakst presented a ballet production, under the direction of Diaghileff, with

Debussy's music, and Nijinski danced as the Faun! It should have been good, and apparently it was. Praised by Rodin, but attacked by the *Figaro*. So the second performance saw a purified version which was attended by the upright police.

Perhaps the most important influence of the poem was on Valéry's *La Jeune Parque* and the two Narcissus poems.

Sainte   page 56

As if to excuse himself for having been naughty, Mallarmé now offers a beautiful little poem, almost pious, as lucent as a sunlit window in Chartres Cathedral. It is written in one sentence, divided by a colon so that the result is a diptych. St. Cecilia would seem to be the subject of the first. Whether what she is concealing be a *viole* or a lute is not the point, because she is not playing it, but points to an old hymnbook, doubtless of vellum, with magnificent rubric and probably square notes in the score. Notice how a far-away-and-long-ago feeling is given by such words as "old," "sandalwood," "mandore," "pale," "once." In the second part the action is sharply concentrated on "balance," and the piece ends with an eternal suspension: an unplayed chord on an unplayable instrument. The saint here is shown against a monstrance window, i.e., a very glittering bit of glazing, though the monstrance proper would be an "ostensoir," a vessel of gold, faced with a sunburst and containing the Host. Mallarmé employs the term to give a feeling of religious dignity and splendor to his poem. She seems to be playing on the spread wing of an angel who is going home at evening. This looks like a large harp, so she playfully "balances" her delicate fingers above the wing and the rest is silence. Truly, "Heard melodies are sweet, but those unheard / Are sweeter." Once—and he stresses the word by using it twice,—once there was music of the Magnificat, a fine hymn, supported with viol, mandore (an instrument like a mandolin), and flute. But a new music, a music of silence, is now suggested.

The rhymes are of two sorts: those with full, open sounds,

like *dédore, mandore, ostensoir, soir,* and the muted nasals, *recélant, étincelant, étalant, ruisselant, Ange, phalange, balance, silence.* It is an effective device for producing unity. The critics either overlooked this piece or, more probably, were afraid they might spoil it by touching. I am glad they did, because it is one of my favorites, and together with the second fan poem it is one of the most delicately conceived of them all.

By way of contrast, notice the beginning of "Vitrail," by Heredia, which opens: "Cette verrière a vu dames et hauts barons / Etincelants d'azur, d'or, de flamme et de nacre . . ." You expect a fine stained-glass window, but the whole poem is concerned with the ladies and nobles, their petty occupations, and their stone effigies on the tombs. It is a fine sonnet, but something very different, with its sonorous words, rich metals, and glittering colors, its mention of falcons and crusades. It is a Parnassian piece, a rather chilly, calm statement. There is nothing haunting or evasive about it.

Toast funèbre   page 58

As usual, Wais, p. 388, is helpfully factual. Catulle Mendès, the son-in-law of Gautier, arranged an obituary testimonial for the dead poet. Heredia, Leconte de Lisle, Coppée, Anatole France, Mallarmé, and others read poems at the funeral, and a book was finally published that included some seventy-five others, one by Swinburne! It was gotten out five years later, 1877, by Lemerre. Because of the hard gemlike quality of his verse (*Emaux et Camées*), Gautier had long been one of the leaders of the Parnassians. There is nothing difficult in the meaning of this elegy, although some of the phrases require investigation.

Thibaudet, p. 54, cites this poem with the "Faun" as those which show "evidence of development." On p. 154 he comments that this piece and the three commemorative sonnets to Poe, Baudelaire, and Verlaine are all of a pattern. The tombs are described, then the man's work, his spiritual self is succinctly evaluated, usually in one unforgettable phrase. Aside from this, he doesn't help much.

The couplets are lapidary, and that would have pleased Gautier, but the piece has a rhetorical rather than poetical feeling about it. The poet knew he would have to read it aloud. Incidentally, he was the chairman of the committee. "L'absence du poète" is a form of euphemism that becomes more and more in evidence in the later poems, until we finally discover an "absence éternelle de lit"! Which makes it really *some* bedroom. Both Mallarmé and Gautier were materialists. "In this great / monument the whole of him is laid. / Unless . . ." Then he goes on to speak of the immortality of the poet's work. Each section is carefully cemented to the next by the simple device of splitting a couplet. The second stanza mentions "le blazon des deuils," which were those diamond-shaped hatchments in vogue during the feudal period when the nobility was particularly conscious about heraldry. These commemorative escutcheons of the donor's coat of arms were sent as a sign of condolence to the family. Many castle halls and stairways are decorated with them throughout countries that took up with chivalry. The poet as "virgin-hero" who has given the rose and lily immortal names returns after death and survives "in a solemn tumult of words on the air." Mallarmé perhaps had himself in mind as much as Gautier when he expressed with such delicate care his wish that the dead poet and his poetry should enjoy renown. Neither of these poets wanted anything to do with the melancholy dreams of a sentimentalized religious immortality. Gautier rests forever in that monumental and massive final line. "In Memoriam" and "Adonais" always seem mediocre poems to me. And we have a sincerity not to be found in Milton's *tour de force*. One of its beauties is that it requires no notes, but speaks directly to the reader.

Prose   page 62

Subtitled "pour des Esseintes," this is very hard going; but it was difficult to please Huysmans's fastidious duke. One must simply read *A Rebours* to get a thorough understanding of the poetry of the period. Probably no other fifty-six lines of French poetry have stimulated such a bulk of *explications* and criticism. I could do no better than to present a digest of several of the commentators. Thibaudet, pp. 403–416, has analyzed the poem—for such, despite its title, a reading will prove it—which is considered to be the essence of unintelligibility. Whoever wishes to ridicule Mallarmé cites a stanza or so, and even the most ardent Mallarméist sees in it but word music, a series of vague images, without exact meaning. (It seems to me a rather indirect statement of what we all know: children have a sense of a vague beauty which is finally lost as they grow older.) The dreamy landscape symbolizes the poet's existence, and this piece is the writer's *Art poétique*.

Stanza 1. Pure poetry is hyperbole. Modern poetry is artificial, composed of memories of an ancient and refined humanity (civilization?) specified in the Byzantine arts, which are preserved "de ma mémoire." The adverb "triomphalement," sprawled out through the fragile octosyllabic verse, as if on a desk, gives it a fullness of authority, as if it were in an ironbound tome.

Stanza 2. This new poetry is a work of *science* (sic), of will, of technique. Spirituel, or Byzantine, hearts are those which dissolve in flames of culture, intellect, and refined voluptuousness which culminate in *A Rebours*. Line 4 refers to the symbols of this patient culture. As in the conclusion of *Candide,* one must learn to cultivate his own garden, although within it grow strange flowers.

Stanza 3. For whom shall one write, this exile of today, lost in his dream? For all? No. But to write is to exist for others. One reader will suffice him, and better than that, one female reader. "For all women," writes Mallarmé in his fashion review, *La Dernière Mode,* No. 1, "love verse as well as perfumes and jewels . . ." All this is addressed to one woman. An obscure personal allusion introducing the theme of "Hérodiade" and the "Après-midi." The same music and words mingle the woman and the poem; the dream of love and the dream of art symbolize each other. This is the Psyche of his poetry, as Beatrice represented that of Dante.

Stanza 4. A quibble over metaphysics and logic which constitute "l'ère d'autorité" (such a period as that in which Aristotle's unities were supposed to be inviolable), a time that prefers poetry without reticence and allusion and grumbles at the poetry which is not clear and is to be realized only little by little.

Stanza 5. (I read here a dig at the scientific desire to name everything, even without understanding it.) But the poet must substitute the suggestive word, for such is the art which dreams. Here is the vision of the ideal poetic landscape.

Stanza 6. The land of the new poetry, of suggestive subjects rather than of created objects, a place of mysterious beauty. The chapter "Puissances de suggestion" in *Divagations* is a comment on this stanza. (God forbid that I should attempt to summarize a chapter of *his* prose!)

Stanza 7. This and the following two stanzas are of a piece, expanding and discharging (*libéré* expresses something like katharsis) the poem. Here, under the "midi" of stanza 4, one beholds the luminous contour of each flower. This is related to "Toast funèbre." In a poem each word must be isolated with a clarity similar to that of those flowers. Here is the connection between the framework of the Parnassians and the fervor of the Symbolists in relation to words (thus Thibaudet).

Stanza 8. This is the climax of the poem: "Gloire du long désir, Idées," the Platonic idea of flowers, finally molded into verbal realism. The first and third lines have an identical four-syllabic rhyme word. This is a dream of the pure poetry in which the poet, hand in hand with his friend, is elated. Then the thought glides away, smiling ironically.

Stanza 9. The smile of the beloved (and I take this to be a composite of the young Harriet and the poet's sister, for we have to do here with a childhood's emotion), like a touch on

134

the shoulder, returns to us at the beginning: "Nous fûmes deux." Two phantoms have entered the solitary garden. The last line of this quatrain has a variant given by the poet to Edmund Gosse: "Je mets mon exotique soin." Less agreeable to the ear, this fits better with the previous stanzas. The poet has substituted for an epithet of space one of duration, of equal value, based on an archaic Byzantine motif.

Stanza 10. But if this silence, this "epoch of authority," triumphs, the "spirit of disputation" attempts out of pity to stop it, for it knows that we have seen everything vanish into the ideal realm which does not exist. Poetry is a lily, too tall, on a stalk of stars.

Stanzas 11 and 12. Mallarmé refuses to touch his pen to this "shore" of platitude "which weeps." He wants the amplitude of space where he feels the joy of a man liberated from Plato's cave as he goes toward the new surprise of the ideal. Shocked by hearing the voice of the vulgar, and by seeing the maps where man, little by little, has marked off the boundaries of the known until the territory of the poet seems no longer to exist, the poet wanders as a stranger. This recalls the image from the "Faun" which "prouve, hélas! que bien seul je m'offrais / Pour triomphe la faute idéale de roses," as ideal as the "sol des cent iris."

Stanzas 13 and 14. This is a dream, the instant of love, the sentimental ironic parade. Here the Byzantine motif recovers its gold background and explains to us the initial meaning of the poem. Huysmans, in *A Rebours,* speaks of Mallarmé as "taking delight in the surprises of the intellect, in visions in his own brain, refining on ideas already fine-spun, grafting Byzantine niceties upon them, perpetuating them in inferences no more than barely indicated by an almost imperceptible thread." This is footnoted by a reference to Gautier's preface to *Les Fleurs du Mal,* on the Byzantine school. From these suggestions Mallarmé developed his aesthetic. The two strange names at first sight give a touch of this "Byzantine finesse." Probably, before the appearance of the poem, they had been born of a tender phantasy in which the lovers called each other secret names. These two have also an etymological taste. The beloved, whose ecstasy before the vision of art has passed into a smile of love, lives now only in the name pronounced, and her word . . . closes the poem. On the tomb is only her name: "Pulchérie." His, "Anastase," was born "for parchments of eternity." Hers will make the tomb smile a little, this tomb of poetry which has not blossomed, of dreams that remain—"Le transparent glacier des vols qui n'ont pas fui." And this "Prose" with its frail stanzas, is it not the "too great lily flower" left alive, alone, from the "dream of a hundred irises"? Here is an arrangement of ballet, décor, and music. The thread of the images rests in the middle of the scholastic commentary (evoked by the name "Anastase"). But instead of monks we have dancers—here is the book, the island, the flowers, the smile, the sea, love—an interior logic, a duration of life, the flesh whose shadow I have thrown on these dry pages. Thus Thibaudet, who concludes, after quoting Mallarmé on the dance: "An abridged writing, but perfect in the crystalline delicacy of its stanzas and the fragile rhymes like goldsmith's work; pure Idea, immortalized on a tomb." And otherwhere, "These are some of the most perfect pages of Mallarmé."

Let us now consider what Wais, pp. 444 ff., has to say. This has been strongly compressed, and you wouldn't know you were reading about the same poem. The poet, Wais maintains, is suffering from the dichotomy between his childhood and his maturity. Ophelia is childhood, innocence, naturalness, and beauty; Polonius is the garrulous schoolmaster, puling in senility, with a dried mind and godless cynicism. Thus had Mallarmé, and in his own language, explained Hamlet, and Wais sees an analogy between these and Pulchérie and Anastase. The poet is judging himself and confessing his faith. The relation to Poe's "Tamerlane," "Eleonora," and the "Dialogue between Monos and Una" is obvious, alleges Wais. The land of lost childhood becomes identified with some womanly gesture in a flowery land of "other days." This is a combination of the Harriet-Ophelia-Pulchérie personalities, just as later life is related to Polonius-Anastase, to which Wais adds the analogy of Faust, before and after his youth was restored. The hothouse rhymes: *devisions–de visions; devoir–de voir; approfondit–motif, on dit,* etc., and the delicate lathe-turned octosyllables resemble the technique of early Christian liturgy. Here is a copper Latinity used with ironic intent. Employing "l'hymne des cœurs spirituels" almost as a charm, to help evoke the memory of childhood, he uses also the para-phernalia of the alchemists and the medieval books of wisdom as aids to magic. (Cf. Soula, *Essai sur l'hermétisme mallar-méen,* pp. 28, 31.) And suddenly he is back in the lost world with this "sister," the feminine half of the *Verschwesterung* (brother-sister relation). A childhood's symphony from mem-ories of Poe and *Paul et Virginie* is evoked, a southern fairy-land. But to this now grown-up pair (Mallarmé seems to insist that the Marie-Harriet composite is not dead) it is unreal. Formerly the flowers were merely a vast growth; the children did not question them or talk about what they saw. The Garden of Eden was a unity. But now, in the called-forth vision, the scientific spirit is awake and must name the flowers "Irides." The sister smiles, the essence of this fulfill-ment, but the brother can no longer partake of that uncon-scious joy of childhood and its silent absorption of beauty. Now they return (so Wais) to the shore (of the mainland), to the bawling instruction of ossified adults and the dull play of the school (*jeu monotone*) which present the lie of some education (*ampleur*) really worth while. And still the child knew that this lost Orplid had existed.

(I am heartily glad he mentions Orplid, for it is my pleasant duty as annotator—like the conscientious Mr. Eames of *South Wind*—to explain Möricke's fairy island. I remember doing this when I was a student in Marburg. When I first found the poem I was in an ectasy all day and never heard a lecture, though I was present.

GESANG WEYLAS

Thou art Orplid, my land
that from afar gleameth;
out of the sea along thy sunny strand,
wetting the cheeks of the Gods, the mist upsteameth.

Old, old waters stealing
about thy hips, O child, grow young again!
Before thy Godhead kneeling,
await the Kings, who are thy servingmen.

I would rather have lived in Orplid than in Mallarmé's
botanical garden.)

The child loses her ecstasy and already become learned
(*docte*), speaks (for the last time *Elle* [*Schwester*], childishly)
the word "Anastasius," he who was born for eternal parch-
ments. With this word of communication, the name with
only one meaning, the still unnamed child (*Ne porte pas de
nom . . .*) *l'enfant* loses her womanly beauty; she will grow
up and become monachal (I am sure he had better used a
word like "conventual," because the other has a masculine
association) and scholarly. Man has created a homeless in-
tellectual being, he has driven out poetry, and he has allowed
only the masculine side of his mind to be important. But
always there is a hope that this split can be healed. Some day
there will be a tomb in some sunny Nowhere, which will
reach far back into the what-has-been. And on the stone the
dull tiresome name of Anastasius will be effaced and the
name of the vanished sister, Pulcheria (Beauty), will be
graven, and the stone will laugh at the idea that this name
of supreme loveliness could appear on any tombstone whatever.
But the grave will be scarcely visible because it will be over-
grown by an unearthly hyperbolic fire lily (German for
orange lily, but this by no means is the same as *glaïeul*). Re-
turning thence to the long-lost cradle of this brother-sister-
hood, this earthly paradise, finally the old yearning of the

138

apostate Mallarmé has again attained a mystical rejuvenation into childhood. He has been reborn: "à renaître . . . au ciel antérieur où fleurit la Beauté." ("Les Fenêtres.")

I can't honestly say that these two exegeses really mean much to me either; the poem has grown into me by many readings, and maybe I can do an explanation on my own some day. Here, I will add only one remark. The concept of the Byzantine influence arising from use of the name Anastase is sound enough, for between the fifth and tenth centuries it was the name of three popes, a patriarch of Antioch, and two emperors of the Eastern Empire. A rereading of the two poems on Byzantium by Yeats will make apparent the Mallarméan implication, for the Irish poet contracted the idea from one of the famous Tuesday evenings in the rue de Rome.

Autre Eventail   page 68

I have elsewhere observed that the triumph of the poet's genius is concealed precisely in his manner of dealing with seemingly trivial things so that they are endowed with an import far greater than their face value. You will notice that better in the short-line last sonnets. But here is a case at hand. The poem is for Geneviève, who was then twenty, a fairly pretty blonde whom Whistler painted in gray and rose—and a charming thing he made of it! The father used to write playful verses on Easter eggs, in red and gold ink; now his grateful love for her leads him to place a scepter in her hand and leave her, graciously poised in eternity. Debussy set the poem to music in 1913. What a threefold bid for artistic immortality the girl has! The fan is whispering to her on a warm summer evening: she is ripe for romance but as yet untouched by it. Any French girl of Mallarmé's social class is usually well protected by a vigilant mother. The play of the fan-strokes creates a microcosm in the slight segment of a circle comprised by its movements. But the poem thrusts forth the radial ribs of the fan until they grow so far apart that only the horizon can put an arc to it. This is the true power of poetry. Now all space trembles, like the great kiss formed invisibly on the girl's wistful lips. But there is no objective for the impulse, so it is turned off into a smile that slips from the corner of her lips into the "unanimous crease," the compact folds of the fan. Then the girl poses its rose and gold, like a little queen's scepter, so that it contrasts with the ruby or garnet bracelet. Very pretty. This is a perfect bijou of playfulness and should not be cluttered with documentation. Yet I must be faithful to Thibaudet, who maintains, p. 111, that it is a pure Mallarméan symbol which reminds him of one of Grimm's fairy tales in which a bird and a stone are tossed into the air; the stone returns, but the bird is lost in the infinite sky. P. 242, he calls it "a periphrase of lacework . . . a masterpiece of the Parnassian goldsmith's art." The pattern comes from the tight octosyllabic verses of Gautier's *Emaux et Camées*. Chisholm, who is better on over-all philosophical background than on individual poems, calls it "the increate form of movement, that factor of musicalization" which he praises so strongly. Wais, p. 498, notices the inverted comparisons of stanza 4 where normally the thought would run "your smile, like a paradise." With typical German sentimentality he reads into the frail verses a symbol of the twilight of maidenhood in which the fan pushes the earth gently away. P. 196: Hence the paradise becomes to him "eine glühende Unschuldswelt"—a glowing world of innocence which overflows into the foldings of the fan.

II

The section of the *Poésies* entitled "Feuillets d'Album" (Album leaves) implies what one may expect: not much. Most of the pieces should have been included in his *Vers de circonstance.*

Feuillet d'album   page 70

This is rather amusing and gently tender and was written to a Mlle Roumanille whom the poet knew as a child. I have not discovered if he really played the flute; the whole piece may be mere blague. Anyway, he pulls off a pretty compliment to an apparently charming young woman, which may have been all he intended. He had rather look at her than hear himself play. Would to God a thousand other musicians felt so! Wais gets heated up about the friends of Mallarmé's daughter and the playful father, et cetera. It is built up of so much nothing, like a fragile pastry of whipped cream. It is artful in the worst sense of the word, a *tour de force*. He should have had a stern editor! (As I have.)

Remémoration d'amis belges   page 72

The swans and canals are the best of the dead city of Bruges; once a large Hanseatic League port, with 200,000 inhabitants, it has shrunk to 50,000 or less. No housing problem there! The bells are vastly overrated. I find them rather tinny. If Mallarmé found geniuses there, they have never been heard of. Thibaudet likes this sonnet. There is, he alleges, a sensuous voluptuousness about these verses that are full of peace and sweetness. Line 4 is particularly good, he insists (p. 269), because it suppresses the classic caesura! I don't think many readers would suffer if the whole sonnet had been suppressed. "Selon" is used in the sense of "en fonction, en harmonie, en suite" (p. 322). M. Thibaudet is often rather a hairsplitter than an interpretative critic.

Chansons bas   page 74

The critics have ignored these eight little jests (of which I give five), although Wais, p. 384, calls them "Tanagra-Figürchen, aus Erde gebrannt." No, they are, rather, comical woodcarvings in the Bavarian style. But some of them have almost the life of characters that flit through Villon's shadowy pages. "Bateleurs traymany marmotes . . . povres housseurs

. . . De Petit Pont deux harengieres . . . vielles sotes / Assises bas, a croupetons, / A petit feu de chenevotes . . . belle Gantiere," and the rest of them. Banville and Coppée liked to write of street types; Daumier has some fine vigorous and humorous sketches of them; Aristide Bruant has preserved two volumes of their songs, naughty little things in argot. Degas's laundresses must have been there from the beginning. Les Halles teems with various types from two in the morning until sunrise.

III. The roadmender is used as an analogy for the school-master's life, or the poet's work, as you will. Mallarmé was well aware of the stony resistance of most of his school pupils, and they had made fun about his poems to the Azure.

IV. There may be more here than a tribute to the social powers of garlic and onions. An importunate caller may cost the world a poet's masterpiece; had Coleridge breathed away the man from Porlock, we should have had the rest of "Kubla Khan." And weepy verses are all too easy for the elegist who keeps, so to say, an onion in his handkerchief—like Lamartine.

V. The quarryman's imagination that will buck him up to propose marriage is so practical; no romantic nonsense here.

VII. The newsboy isn't necessarily a mere Gavroche-gamin; all sorts of cripples, dopes, old men, and crones sell papers in France. Imagine what Eugene Field would have done with him!

VIII. The old-clo' dealer shrewdly appraises the poet's suit as he walks past; apparently he feels rather apologetic about it himself, for he shudders to be left stripped by her derisive eyes.

As a group of vignettes, the effect of these small pieces is rather amusing, but they, too, should have been printed in Mallarmé's volume of light verse. One realizes how patheti-cally little the poet had to show for a life of painstaking labor. The book contains probably fifteen hundred lines, and of these barely half are really pure Mallarméan. How many of them will survive a hundred years is a question, but the contemporary effect has been far beyond what might be expected from the slender quantity.

Petit Air   page 78

With the two pieces under this title we enter the real world of Mallarméan obscurity. Here he becomes purposely difficult and chooses to loosen a few drifting bits of gossamer to dazzle the eye as they drift past. But they are not wholly without meaning if one reconstructs them logically. I shall attempt the first air. The scene is no doubt the Seine, for the poet was very fond of the river and later had a small house beside it and sailed a little yawl on Sundays. The banks are flat and uninteresting. But on this occasion the ostentation of the sky with its "bariole," stripped, effect, is equally boring—until the woman appears. The white linen she sheds, in a delicate strip tease, either scares some bird, or is the bird metaphorically. Then she dives into a wave that becomes, is, actually the naked girl. "Gloriole" in French has no religious connotation. Let us judge these slight verses from the point of view expressed by Diderot when he observed to Mlle Voland: "Une seul qualité physique peut conduit l'esprit qui s'en occupe à une infinité de choses diverses." Here is another "pretext for reverie." After all, this nude natation might develop into an amusing finale.

The second little air gets off, after a thundering adverb. Unconquerably, indomitably, leaps the hope of the poet into the air, even as the bird's song, which at once is identified with that of the poet. The strange song will not be heard again in this life, and we can be assured of that. There will be no second Mallarmé. In the third quatrain the difficulty always implicit between two languages shows up. "Hagard" meant in Old French a hawk captured when adult which could never be tamed, hence wild, savage. How the word went astray in English to mean "gaunt" is a mystery. It is useless to attempt to keep the connotation of true wildness in the English. But it means, rather, one strayed from the normal way of civilization. This could hardly apply properly to the poet, who was essentially a very urbane and civilized person. But he seems to fancy himself here as a wild spirit. So the bird wonders if maybe the poet's pains aren't as bad as its own, or worse. What will its fate be, who knows? The poem is very light and musical and reminds one not at all of any English bird poems. Thibaudet, pp. 123–125, reports that Mallarmé liked negative words, but I fail to see how that helps us further. The little poem remains, as it were, in suspension above a dream horizon.

III

Now we arrive at the third section, the most famous, and the best, as far as I'm concerned: "Plusieurs Sonnets." Probably his future reputation could rest safely here, even though the "Faun" and "Hérodiade" were lost.

Le vierge, le vivace et le bel aujourd'hui   page 82

This is the sitting duck for all teachers of advanced French courses. "Es klingt so wundersam!" The cold white imagery pleases the little girls' hearts and they sympathize so with the poor swan. Maybe the presence of the *i*-sound at the end of every line and the more than a dozen *v*'s—Poe said the *v*-sound was the most beautiful because it is heard in *v*iolets and *v*iols—all helped. I've asked a score of these little twiddlers and all they remember is the cold bird. Aside from this, it presents another dichotomy of the two worlds, and the poet immediately identifies himself with the swan by "nous." Frozen in the winter of his often admitted sterility, he feels hopeless "Pour n'avoir pas chanté la région où vivre," or because, as Thibaudet quotes from an earlier version, he has turned his shoulder to life "Pour n'avoir *connu*," etc. He has not been able to sing forth his own escape, as did Gauguin, say, who threw everything to the winds and strode into his destiny. The obscurity of the first two lines will partly be lighted if one remembers that the day must be the subject of "tear," hence, a thaw is implied, and "ivre" does not necessarily imply intoxication. I suppose the bird was beating his wings, too, but grammar is grammar. But whether or not the victim be released, he has been assigned this place by his "pur éclat"—one's character is one's fate. White bird, white snow. In his futile exile the bird proudly awaits his destiny. In no possible way could a translator get fourteen end words on one rhyme. The French don't care how often a rhyme sounds identical. To my ear, "nie–agonie, assigne–Cygne" are no rhymes at all; but it's his poem. He has left us a little symphony of ivory, white snow, and golden sunlight, in which the immobile white bird sits as on a throne. Gautier wrote up a real incident from the Tuileries: "Un cygne s'est pris en nageant / Dans le bassin des Tuileries . . ." and Baudelaire has a line: "Un navire pris dans le pôle / Comme en un piège de cristal." Nothing like a bit of stimulation from one's predecessors. I think the Buddha would have understood this poem completely as an ideal of fate and wise passiveness.

Victorieusement fui le suicide beau   page 82

I have too long put off an explanation of Méry (or Mary) Laurent. Wais, pp. 197–204, positively drools over the story. Here are the essentials from various sources. According to the Count Montesquious, she was "one of the last great courtesans of the Second Empire." This alone is great praise, for think what a deal of competition she must have had, and with all the young amateurs coming along, too! But one must remember Castiglione's definition of the term: she was the concomitant to his famous courtier, who was the ideal of little Sir Philip Sydney. The term implies, rather, that she demanded brains instead of money from her lovers. A wealthy dentist, an American, had set up a ménage for her in Paris—and had probably fixed her teeth. She was discovered at an exhibition of Manet's paintings by the painter himself, who was pleased with some astute comment she made. He promptly annexed her, in 1876, and she soon became a favorite among a circle of Bohemians, including Villiers, Becque, Coppée, and Régnier, who introduced her finally, in 1888, to Mallarmé—she seems to have pretty well completed the rounds before this, however. During the interval she was no doubt making cultural inquiries and studies so that her intellectual maturity kept pace with what a dozen years can do to a socially active woman, and she was all groomed and ready for her last *maître*. Manet's portrait of her, in a dark fur hat, collar, and muff, all very subdued, nevertheless reveals a woman of esprit with a sensitive mouth, and not fat! That she was elegant, witty, good-natured, understanding, is taken for granted. The picture of her parlor is chuck-full of all the bad taste of the period, but she needn't be blamed for that. There was no standard of taste just then. One must smile to imagine how Mallarmé's soul must have shuddered at the décor! But she rented a summer-house where she and her new friend could sit in an ivy garden and discuss literature to the twittering of the little birds. She is the heroine of an episode in *Divagations,* "Déclaration foraine," in which she put on a fashion show at an unpopular booth in a fair, while the poet acted as impromptu barker and related the lady's charms. Apparently, without song or dance, she was a success, for Mallarmé gleefully relates that a young officer in the audience slipped off his gloves in "l'estimation d'une jarretière hautaine," plotting against a garter high on a gam. In the present sonnet he pokes fun at himself for having melodramatically considered the joys of self-destruction against such a fine theatrical sunset as background. He enjoys the conceit that the sun is spreading a pall of crimson splendor over his "absent tombeau," a typical negative. Then night falls, and the confusion of loosened hair becomes the catalytic that precipitates the new verses. The "festive shade" is doubtless an intimate little dinner party in the ivy garden. Her hair is so luminous that it does famously without any other light, for has she not wound some of the sun's glory along with the childish triumph she has braided in her hair? But suddenly this becomes a royal helmet, a casque of golden gleams, from which pours forth the rose stream of a naked body. I refuse to accept any ideas about a pink lawn garden dress. Thus a solar phenomenon has become a limited private experience. She can be an empress for all I care, if Mallarmé thinks of her that way; for, as Anatole France discreetly observed, "Some women are queens when they yield themselves."

Ses purs ongles très haut dédiant leur onyx   page 84

This can only be called "arty," in the most pejorative sense. A *tour de force* based on two rhymes, and one of them he has to make up a word for, it indicates what he meant when he told Degas that poems weren't written with ideas, but with words. But there is a frail thread of idea throughout. The *-yx* rhymes are amusing and the *-ore* sounds are always impressive. But it's merely bad baroque art, at that, a trick almost unworthy of him. Wais, p. 405, states that night is the lamp bearer. I disagree, for the rare punctuation and the capitalization of "Angoisse" immediately make it the subject. One must envision an elaborate statue holding an onyx translucent bowl in her fingertips, which thus become the same radiant material. This anguish is the misery of the poet's noncreative period, during which his unwritten poems may be said to have been burned. Aside from the lamp and bearer, the credenzas, the room is empty. No bibelots—I read here a reaction against Méry's stuffed-full parlor—or tricks. The Greek word πτύξ, as in Pindar's *Olymp.* I, 105, means "a fold." Apparently it has here been forced to mean a rhyme that folds back on itself, like two pages of a book, an identical rhyme. This probably refers to those pat rhymes of Gautier and Banville and the Parnassians who went in for *rimes riches*. This device our poet considered to be outmoded and "full of sound and fury." But with his usual preference for his own tenuous unrealities, he turns to the window, giving on the north, which allows him to see Ursa Major. Just how the pale light of the Dipper can illuminate any décor on a north wall is beyond me. The poor little nixie—like the girl in St. James' Infirmary, "so cold, so white, so bare"—is being spurned by the unicorns, always guardians of virginity, because the very charm of her form seems to have led her astray. If the mirror were on the north wall and the plaque of mythical figures on the south wall, and rather close to the floor, at that, one can see then that the glittering of the décor might appear in the mirror. I still think I can't take it. The sestet may relate, as a minor addition, to the theme of the octave: the folded rhymes of the dead Master, rhymes and form that do honor to the Nothingness behind creation (for Mallarmé)—it may be that her very "form," as a part of the Parnassian theory, is here attacked by the righteous unicorns of chastity. I believe a definite pause should be indicated after "miroir," and the concluding clause should read: "Now, in the window frame, the septet, with all its shining, is fixed." In this, as in so many of the other poems, the pleasure and the irritation balance each other. But I can assure a more casual reader that if you once get the hang of it, you don't forget it.

Sonnet   page 86

Now we come to various "Hommages et Tombeaux." My two critics have little to say about this one, but it is certainly the most moving, most easily understood, and most sincere poem thus far. I can find nothing about its *raison d'être,* but the date is that of the day after Toussaint, the Memorial Day of France on which one can see hundreds of mourners going to the cemeteries with flowers, vases, wire frames on which to make arrangements, and a few extra handkerchiefs so they can indulge themselves in the annual lachrymal offering. The returned spirit of the dead wife is speaking to the grieving husband who sits beside the hearth, gazing vacantly at the empty armchair. Perhaps he forgot to take the usual flowers and lamented this to Mallarmé; at any rate, the shade of the dead wife assures him thus: "Don't worry about it, my dear. You've been sitting in a vigil all evening—why, it's long past bedtime—and I've been here beside you, just as of old, only you couldn't see me. Moreover, if you had put too many flowers on my tombstone, I wouldn't have been able to lift it and get out to come see you. Remember this, that all you ever need do, if you want me to visit you, is to murmur my name. Then suddenly I'm with you again!" This reads like a fine human poem, a tribute to real grief, and it does make those other *tours de force* look like literary exercises, which they are. Lines 3 and 4 are typical litotic Mallarméisms. The poem gains its power from the concrete sensory suggestions. One can see or hear something in every phrase, there is real feeling behind it, and anyone can understand it. Thus it conforms to Milton's definition: "simple, sensuous, and passionate."

Le Tombeau d'Edgar Poe   page 88

"Not without honor save in his own country" might well be the caption of this sonnet, for Poe's death, in 1849, was followed next year by Rufus Griswold's vicious *Memoir* of the poet, and the grave waited until 1875 for a monument which was, according to Swinburne, "an impossible and trans-Atlantic deformity." It was then that this poem was read— and certainly understood by no man who heard it for the first time—together with tributes from Tennyson, Swinburne, and others, at the dedication. Mallarmé's admiration for Poe has also been attested by his prose translations of some of the poems. But since most of them depend on their word music anyhow, but little of the real magic haunting quality is carried over. There had been other attacks on America's mistreatment of the poet by Baudelaire and Barbey d'Aurevilly, who called it "a revenge of bourgeois mediocrity." Since this is the first of three similar poems, take Thibaudet's word for it, p. 212, that they "summarize and symbolize the work of each poet in an emblematic landscape," as setting.

The first stanza seems to mean: At last now eternity has

given to Poe the real Himself, as he really was always, and the blind dumb people are now startled at discovering that his strange voice was really important. Second: He suddenly appears like an angel, purifying the common language of the folk, and public resentment at being improved at all jerked like a dragon confronted by the avenger, and said his magic came from alcohol. The figure of the angel may come from his own Israfel, who "sang so wildly well," or from the figures of St. George or Michael who spent a deal of time in the Dark Ages slaying dragons, wyverns, cockatrices, basilisks, and a few hydras. The sestet brings in the tombstone, fallen from some dark disaster, as if from the clouds. If Mallarmé by "notre idée" cannot carve a suitable bas-relief, yet may the stone itself set a boundary, for the future, past which no buzzards of blasphemy can dare to come.

I am indebted to Professor W. T. Bandy, of the University of Wisconsin, for pointing out to me the first text, as it is found in a collection of tributes to the dead poet, *Edgar Allan Poe: A Memorial Volume,* put together by Sara Sigourney Rice (Baltimore: Turnbull Brothers, 1877), p. 93. It reads as follows (I italicize words that differ from those of the later version, and replace a few acute accents that were lost by Miss Rice or the printer):

Tel qu'en lui-même enfin l'éternité le change,
Le poëte suscite avec un *hymne* nu
Son siècle épouvanté de n'avoir pas connu
Que la mort *s'exaltait* dans cette voix étrange:

Mais, comme un vil *tressant* d'hydre, oyant jadis l'ange
Donne un sens plus pur aux mots de la tribu,
Tous pensèrent entre eux le sortilège bu
Chez le flot sans honneur de quelque noir mélange.

Du sol et de *l'éther* hostiles, ô grief!
Si *mon* idée avec ne sculpte un bas-relief
Dont la tombe de Poe éblouissante s'orne,

Sombre bloc *à jamais* chu d'un désastre obscur,
Que ce granit du moins montre à jamais sa borne
Aux *vieux* vols *de* blasphême épars dans le futur.

Mallarmé sent to Sarah Helen Whitman (to whom Poe once proposed marriage) his own translation into English, to assist Mrs. Whitman's attempt at an English rendering. Mallarmé's translation with his appended footnotes, which may be found in Caroline Ticknor's *Poe's Helen* (New York: Charles Scribner's Sons, 1916), reads:

Such as into himself at last Eternity changes him,
The Poet arouses with a naked [1] hymn
His century overawed not to have known
That death extolled itself in this[2] strange voice:

But, in a vile writhing of an hydra, (they) once hearing the Angel [3]
To give[4] too pure a meaning to the words of the tribe,
They (between themselves) thought (by him) the spell drunk
In the honourless flood of some dark mixture.[5]

Of the soil and the ether (which are) enemies, O struggle!
If with it my idea does not carve a bas-relief
Of which Poe's dazzling[6] tomb be adorned,

(A) Stern block here fallen from a mysterious disaster,
Let this granite at least show forever their bound
To the old flights of Blasphemy (still) spread in the future.[7]

---

[1] naked hymn means when the words take in death their absolute value.

[2] this	"	his own.
[3] the Angel	"	the above said Poet.
[4] to give	"	giving.
[5] ————	"	in plain prose—charged him with always being drunk.
[6] dazzling	"	with the idea of such a bas-relief.
[7] Blasphemy	"	against Poets, such as the charge of Poe being drunk.

My own translation was made before I had this material, nor do I see much reason to change it. The faults and actual mistakes in Mallarmé's English version are obvious. I take exception particularly to his translation in line 9 of "grief" as "struggle." There are, I believe, several words in French that imply "struggle," and I can no more allow him to mistranslate this word than to call a table a turnip. He goes too far. Lines 9 and 10 are very deliberately awkward, as he has written them. It seems to me that in plain English he means, despite his miserably bungled up French, something like this: Alas, if from the opposing earth and sky our concept cannot make an ornament for the poet's tomb! then at least may this protest warn off future attacks against poets. (Cf. that of the Rev. Mr. Griswold.)

Le Tombeau de Charles Baudelaire   page 90

Baudelaire died in 1867. The greatest poet of France must have a monument, and at once! So, in 1892, *La Plume,* which seems to have been particularly astute and prompt about such matters, appointed a committee: Mallarmé, Heredia, Leconte de Lisle, Verlaine, Verhaeren, Huysmans, Stefan George, and others—a committee of genius if there ever was one. With the celerity characteristic of such bodies, plans were made and briskly pushed, and nine years later the monument was finished—thirty-four years late. The tomb itself is some distance away from the site of the monument. Mallarmé was describing some plan, real or imaginary; it is possible that he had seen one. And the poem is misnamed. A figure swathed in wrappings, like a mummy, but with the head bare, is stretched on a slab a few inches above the ground. A stele rises behind, and on the top of this the upper half of a figure that reminds one of "The Thinker" gazes gloomily at the effigy. A bat or lizardlike creature is crawling up the stele. It is really quite monstrous in its effect. I prefer to pay my homage to the unassuming tomb, under which other members of the family are also buried, one above another. Occasionally, at Toussaint, I have found a small bunch of flowers or so, and have several times left one myself; but I prefer to sit there and read some of the poems. But that awful monument! Nothing in Forest Lawn or Mount Auburn could be worse.

Thus Mallarmé describes an imaginary monument, to his liking. It interests me that he could have been in the grave-yard by lamplight, for the cemeteries are always closed at six o'clock in summer and at five in winter. And how could he have seen that gas lamp? Or maybe the walls are a recent erection. Anyhow, Anubis, the jackel-headed Egyptian god that leads the soul off to judgment, is appropriate enough, for Baudelaire liked to write about wolves. Mallarmé gets his muck and rubies from "Le Vin des chiffoniers":

> Souvent, à la clarté rouge d'un réverbère
> Dont le vent bat la flamme et tourmente le verre,
> Au cœur d'un vieux faubourg, labyrinthe fangeux
> Où l'humanité grouille en ferments orageux...

Mallarmé probably saw the sunken grave before the tomb was installed. No, it's older than that. They certainly can't shove a ton of stone aside, to open a grave. I'm at a loss about what he saw. All critics agree that the lamp with the besotted twisted wick represents the attacks made on the book, the "opprobres subis," by the government and some of the critics. "Cities without evening" would be cemeteries, of course. But the dead poet needs no wreaths of homage, because his Shade seems to brood there. The poison is the effect of the *Fleurs du Mal,* and it is "tutelary" because the complete effect of the book is a deadly morality.

Not much poetry of value has been written since the deaths of Rilke, Valéry, Yeats, Rimbaud, Lorca, George, but cer-tainly all those men had felt the influence, and the whole course of poetry has been changed since 1857. I do not speak of English poetry in the Tennysonian tradition; not a little of that pious saccharinity still trickles occasionally in London.

According to Thibaudet, pp. 308–309, this and the last one
are the most obscure of all. Nor did I need him to tell me
that. Otherwise, he is not at all helpful here. But let us tackle
it together. Remember the solid block for Poe, and the sunken
sewer mouth for Baudelaire. Here we find an angry rolling
rock, which is really a cloud. It may symbolize the poet's life
of vagaries, or it might be the pattern of all lives; but the
excellent Charles Mauron (Fry, pp. 224–228) maintains that
the black rock is this very cloud of religious beliefs and the
idea of sin. The "pious hands are those of Christ, on a cross,
extended in the sky." That's fetching it pretty far, but I
agree with him that "nubiles" offers difficulties. I take it that
the cloud represents Verlaine's stormy hell-bent quality,
angry at being stopped. The pious—here the word is used in
a condemnatory sense—are those godly people who wanted to
make a type of lost sinner from Verlaine's example. Yet the
voice of one true mourner, the stock type of elegiac dove,
seems to make a cloud that hides the poet's star that tomor-
row the mob will understand. Fry, p. 221, translates "nubiles"
as "nubile," which affords no light at all. That means "mar-
riageable," and although Rilke, too, and even, was led astray
on that same path, they're wrong. Mallarmé was a Latinist
of parts, and his tricky little brain wouldn't let him do any-
thing the easy way. He means the word in its Latin sense,
"clouds." These naughty boys have been trying so hard to
find sex symbols in the folds of the clouds! In stanza 1 when
he says "rock" he means "cloud." Here he says "cloudy
folds," but don't clouds often look as if they'd either been
folded or wrinkled? To proceed. If anyone wants to find Ver-
laine now, who has just made one of his usual side leaps
"extérieur," it will be on the bank of a shallow stream that
wasn't so bad as it has been named. The poet is at peace and
does not drink deeply of death. He merely dreams, at ease for
once in his harassed existence.

Maurice Beaubourg has a paragraph in his article "La Toussaint" that I must quote: "Et la famille, se rapprochant soudain, lut au-dessous de deux autres inscriptions vulgaires: 'Nicolas-A. Verlaine, capitaine, et Elisa-Stéphane-Julie Dehée, son épouse,' celle vraiment si troublante dans sa simplicité, de:

PAUL VERLAINE

POETE

MORT LE 8 JANVIER 1896, A 51 ANS!

—Qu'était-ce, . . . Verlaine? . . . , demanda Sophie . . ."

I have written elsewhere of Verlaine's tomb: it is a memory that I would not just here stir up again.

Hommage page 94

Thibaudet, p. 307, calls this "a sonnet of transition, very classically composed," and I immediately beg to differ. The essence of classicism is intelligibility and sobriety; this is willfully obfuscated and melodramatic. It is not only bad poetry, but bad musical judgment. The only accurate phrases in it are "frisson familier" (the old familiar shudder one feels when he knows he's in for the Pilgrims' Chorus or that orgiastic Love-Death scene), "souriant fracas" (if anyone can produce a cacophonic hullabaloo, it's Wagner), "pâmé" (fainting, in its worst sense), and "sanglots" (those eternal wailings and agonies his fat heroines and heroes undergo). It's a very bad poem.

It says, in its twisted fashion: 1. Wagner is dead, the house of his art is draped with funereal palls; tomorrow his fame will be forgotten and sink. 2. But all our old music, with its familiar strains and tricks that make quiver the riffraff, you can stick that away in some old clothespress. 3. The crowd did not take to Wagner at first, but the very bulk of his loud brass makes everybody feel faint and sentimental. 4. Then out hops Wagner, grinning like a Chessy cat, feeling himself a god being anointed. Even the ink of a bad press can't quite

155

choke off those last prophetic sobbings: that his music will still go on for a while—an evil prophecy!

Wais, p. 205, thinks that Mallarmé saw in poetry "the synthesis of all the arts," an idea common to Wagner, especially as concerning his operas. Well and good—if it could be done. But in Wagner's works the setting (architecture) and the noisy music completely dominate the words (poetry), and I've never yet seen a Wagnerian singer with the charm, beauty, or figure that would permit an aspiration toward producing any of the beauty of dance and ballet. Now in Mozart's operas everything is balanced: actors, poetry, light music, and modest décor; grace and restraint are combined; these fulfill the definition mentioned by Wais.

Au seul souci de voyager page 96

Whatever may have been the occasion for this sonnet, its first line reminds one vividly of the voyage undertaken in "Salut." And this gives a keynote to the understanding of Vasco. He is a symbol of the man who "follows his gleam" (Tennyson). Stubbornly, with helm set, the navigator has his vision fixed on a place "outre [*beyond*] une Inde splendide." Something above material treasures, for which India stood to the contemporaries of the hero. Probably Mallarmé has overemphasized the spiritual qualities of the traveler. That matters nothing here. Line 11 I remember seeing mistranslated by either Fry or Fowlie, probably by both—I have lost the notes. "Gisement" was misread as meaning "a lode vein of mineral." The true meaning here is the nautical definition: coastal bearing. That makes sense. It comes from "gésir," and means the "lie," the "position," of the ship. It is a fine synopsis of trouble, that "nuit, désespoir et pierrerie," and it is from the ironic glitter of precious stones he is never to gather that the mariner's pale determined face is lighted. Stanza 2 is a fine description of a ship's movements. In fact, the whole thing goes off so well that the reader forgives *a priori* the tough ones coming up.

Beginning innocently enough as genial advice from an experienced cigar smoker to a neophyte, this slight, unpunctuated sonnet soon shows itself as a little *ars poetica*. It declares the author's aversion to reality, the too precise language of the Parnassians, and is virtually a manifesto of Symbolism. Line 10 has a pun on "vole-t-il" and the implied "volatil." It is inferior to the same poem by Verlaine. The would-be poet must shake off the ashes of the real to keep his small fire glowing. Each new ring puffed out tends to dissipate its predecessor; thus poetry moves and does not remain static. "Vague littérature" is the master's own style and he liked it. Wais, p. 357, calls the present item "a lightfooted weightless poem in the style of the Elizabethan sonnet." Manet has a picture of the poet smoking. Perhaps it was this habit from which he developed a cancer in the throat from which he died. But then, that French tobacco! These short-lined sonnets are very tricky and allow the translator no leeway of selection, but they are fun to try.

Triptych   page 100

I must take this arbitrary title for the moment to discuss as a whole the three parts beginning the "Autres Poëmes et Sonnets." After painstakingly noting Soula's blow-by-blow account, lack of space forces me to cut it. After many years of renewed puttering with these three as a unity, I shall say that they mean to me as follows:

I. Looking around the room at evening, the poet, who is really there—although he appears not to have come in yet,—feels chilly. The lacking fire may be supposed to purport warmth of understanding and applause. The bygone trophies, the petty triumphs en route, seem a mockery. The only gleam in the room comes from the brass claw-feet of the console table, which has a black marble top that reminds him of the tomb. I'll come to individual lines later.

II. Here the poet speaks as if he were the chilly sylph on

the ceiling. The glass chandelier with swan's-neck curve springs from the croup, the base of the supporting rod from the ceiling. The mother is the glass flower or cup at the end, and the lover is the absent candle, fire, desire, or what you will. These seem to have been the parents of the dispossessed one who mournfully regards the lightlessness. But the receptacle, the "pur vase," has an eternal widowed doom; i.e., the lover—in this case, the poet's inspiration—comes no more. So there is no rose in the cup, no kiss, no poem, in the poet's sterile brain.

III. A pair of lace curtains is blown by a breeze, wreathing around each other like lovers. There is no bed, or rather, there is an eternal absence of bed, but you can't stop two amorous curtains, not in a Mallarméan huddle, you can't! The supreme game probably refers to poetry. Now, the sestet: Here broods the dreamy poet, with his *mandore* (mandola, mandoline), his instrument for making poetry, sorrowfully, in a silence that is empty. Now then, he seems to be thinking, if I could only impregnate, fertilize by parthenogenesis, as it were, myself, I could conceive, beget, sire and mother, a son of my own, a poem. Line 12 seems to mean that if he alone could do what the curtains are doing by the pane, the pane meaning also the source of light and creation, why, then he would be self-sufficient and happy.

The three poems have followed: (1) in the evening room where the only fire was a mocking gleam, (2) in the night vigil above an unlighted rose, he has been hunting the right poetic stimulus. But fire and light availed him nothing. At dawn he turns to the idea of music: auditory, rather than visual stimulus, would turn the trick. He has shown the vagaries of poetic search, the doodling of the artist, the improvisings of a musician idly fingering keys, until inspiration has come, and in passing he has produced his poem. As a composite unified about one subject these three sonnets seem highly successful, and not so very tough, at that. Reread with this idea of unity, they readily fall in with the reader, but he mustn't fight them over trivialities.

Now, if we must, here they are singly, with critica.

Tout Orgueil fume-t-il du soir   page 100

Thibaudet, p. 46, says that Mallarmé "strove to endow the furniture of his house with a quality of subtle essence, and to paint it with the care of a Metzu and the mystery of a Carrière." Wais, pp. 407 ff., sees in the shaken torch the symbol of the aging poet's anticipation of death. Soula, *Essai,* p. 67, wonders if the "dying fire"—now where does he get that from?—doesn't symbolize the passing of human glory.

Surgi de la croupe et du bond   page 100

Mauron (Fry, p. 257) laments: "There is no such thing as complete union." So we'll have to bear up with the unlit candle in the widowed vase. Soula insists on seeing a flowerless vase; moreover, he sees it a "vase brisé," like that cracked pot of Sully-Prudhomme's, which schoolgirls weep over: a poor little vase was broken by the blow of a fan, and all the water has trickled away, drop by drop, and the sap of the little flower, alas, is now exhausted! You see, that's what happens to professors of physiology who want to kick up their heels in Hyblean meadows, like Sancho Panza's donkey. Although it may *look* intact (thus, in his text) to everyone, the wound is so deep and too small to be seen—I should hope so. So the vase just cracks away silently and dies a chilly porcelain china-closet death. Zut alors! I like to think of the sylph as a disembodied spirit wishing to be born, as in Buddhist countries those who have died young are supposed to lurk constantly around any two lovers and give them little spirit nudges to bring them to the desirable propinquity. So they'll have a chance, at least.

Une dentelle s'abolit page 102

Thibaudet, p. 113, maintains that here the poet finds in absence "an equivalent aesthetic of silence." Remember the musician of silence. P. 136, he quotes Remy de Gourmont: "Mallarmé is capable, and he alone, of imagining a phrase representative of an absence of images." Sometimes I get so annoyed that I have to write something like this: A man afflicted with wifelessness is trying to sleep in a room equipped with perpetual unscreenlessness, in a continual unabsence of non-unstingless mosquitos who bite the unscratchableness of his unwifelessly tended back. Matter of fact, Scarron did dream once of "an absence of coachman who with the idea of a brush would scrub a vacancy of carriage." Mauron (Fry, p. 264) insists that the second quatrain really implies "burying," which "would seem only to allow of the interpretation, the burying of a seed, fecundation" . . . Dear me! I had no idea such things went on, and with sleazy Nottingham curtains, too. Really, his note affords quite a literary orgy; but then, M. Mauron is French. The charming thing about the French language is that "ventre" is masculine, and in this case "le sien" seems to clinch that. Soula reads into the sestet the notion that the hollow mandolin is a universe freed from the flight of time, saddened by the impossible art sought by its poet. The window's light stands, he says, for hope and faith. He also thinks that "the white conflict" of the curtains has impregnated the mandola. As Anatole France more justly observed: "What shall be said of the charming immoralities among the flowers?"

Quelle soie aux baumes de temps page 104

Mallarmé is here again lost in his usual hirsute obsession. "Tangled in Neaera's hair," Milton has it. A military parade is passing, with meditative banners, that is, the banners make one meditate on the folly of war. The Chinese silk with dragon emblazoned was probably a boudoir hanging. Nothing was past Méry! The poet, in common, I suppose, with

most artists—well, men in general,—never tires of watching
the woman arrange her hair. One must take such verse with
this idea, from Sainte-Beuve in the Preface of his *Consola-
tions:* "Le but de l'art est de déterminer chez le lecteur une
émotion esthétique, qui à son tour créera une série d'émotions
suggestive." But that "considérable touffe," he has used else-
where. What a description of the crowning glory! With his
nose buried in the girl's hair, he forgets the cries of stifled
calls of Glory. That is one way out.

M'introduire dans ton histoire page 106

In my darkest hours since I began this project, in 1939, and
there have been many, I have always found some consolation
in Thibaudet, who is sometimes illuminating, often stimulat-
ing, and betimes amusing. P. 77; here I find: "The Chinese,
it appears, call the bicycle a little mule which one makes go
by holding onto his ears and kicking him in the belly. To use
this means of transportation is, according to M. Mallarmé, 'to
roll between one's hams, along the road . . . the fiction of a
shining continuous rail.'" Then I read in Wais, pp. 430–431,
that "he was a favorite of Méry Laurent, and was worried
lest he cast a shadow over her world of pleasure. So he de-
signed this poem as her introduction into his idea of beauty
and his shy nature. And he asks her if she can't see that he
has fun in thinking of the sunset as a vast carriage wheel
with ruby-spraying naves." Really now, I wish I still had
Herr Wais's naïve innocence, I really do. There is a quotation
from *La Presse,* cited in Wais's notes: "One must be de-
praved to understand the hidden meaning of such a poem as
(the present one)." Now I am in a dilemma: Either I don't
understand it, or I'm depraved. Let me bulwark our tottering
morals by hastening to quote from Charles Mauron (Fry,
pp. 278–280): It would be stupid "not to see the rôle played
by the erotic feeling untinged by morbidity . . . Mallarmé's
audacity in this direction could go to real crudity, as in the
poem 'Une négresse par le démon secouée.' After all, this is

as ancient as literary tradition, and even the austere Malherbe advised his pupils to practise erotic compositions." He then goes on to observe that "histoire" can mean any of several things. The title means, of course, "to take a place in your existence, but the nature of the intrusion is not left in doubt." A footnote follows this: "In colloquial French *histoire* is much vaguer than 'story' and can mean any sort of object."

The frightened hero reminds me that des Esseintes, believing in the aphrodisiacal effect of fear, hired a ventriloquist who, even in his arms, could play the angry husband outside the door. At any rate, the lover here is timid, although he claims to have ravished glaciers. This girl seems to have him under control. Well, since she is less attainable than even a glacier, he resigns himself to playing games with the sunset which he sees conventionally as a chariot, but with fine thunder and rubies clean to the axles, and to watch the dying crimson of the sinking sun, as the only form of worship he is to attend that evening. Thibaudet, p. 301, mentions that the concluding two lines are an enigma, like all the last sonnets. Mauron has it that Valéry, quite a dealer in enigmas himself, suggested that the couple were riding in a buggy with red wheels! Wais, p. 431, has it, "The evening sun-chariot, as we know, was to him the expression of the loftiest earthly beauty." But whatever the wheel may be, Mauron concludes his note drily: "After all, one only has the triumphs that one can."

A la nue accablante tu page 108

Since the critics have ignored or avoided this little sonnet— nor do I blame them,—I feel forced to defend it. For I have worked so often and long on it that, to save my face, I must believe it good for something, save being a brain whetter. There is no punctuation to help, but the octave and sestet are separated by the "ou" of line 9. The massive basalt-like cloud of disaster has muted the cries of the shipwrecked sailors, even the weakly blown horn, calling for help, and has muffled

162

the noise of the crash. Only the foam left as the tempest subsides knows how the mast fell. And only the foam knows, too, that in its so white trailing bubbles an innocent young siren was drowned. Lines 9 and 10 may mean that the ocean has failed to make a really "high perdition," a first-class wreck. The visual qualities of the slight piece are so restrained and few that the economic effect heightens their power. The crushing cloud, hovering over, or synonymous with, the the basalt-and-lava cliff, the falling mast, the vast abysm, with white foam-trails around it, and the final pathetic drowned siren-child, a sad cold little nude, probably tossed on the beach. Yet the reader seems to have some disaster of far vaster import than he can fathom. That is the mysterious effect of Mallarmé's poetry. One gets a strange emotional effect past analysis.

Mes bouqins refermés sur le nom de Paphos   page 110

Poets are always very careful about choosing the first and last poem of a volume. Why was just this one chosen? Here sits Mallarmé, his feet on an andiron shaped like a mythological wyvern, something like a cockatrice. He is surrounded by his books. Outside, the wind is blowing loose snow sharply across the ground. Everything about the poem deals with something finished, dead, negative, nonexistent, fabulous, or in some way or other unreal. His books are *old,* they are *closed,* and on the name of a *dead* city. He chooses a *ruin,* past its triumphant days. Let the *cold* scythelike wind blow the snow off and reveal the naked earth, it has spoiled everything for him by making the landscape *too real.* His hunger that will feast on *no* fruits here finds in their *absence* an *indifferent* taste, although one of them, probably his wife, warm human flesh, bursts with yearning for a bit of attention. Feet on a *wyvern* where love stirs the fire, he broods longer *desperately,* on the *ancient Amazon's seared* breast.

He is satisfied with nothing present, real, or human, but wants the far-away, the defunct, the unreal landscape. He

163

wants some absent fruit, the nonexistent Amazon's lost breast. For she had sacrificed it, you remember, to increase her skill as a toxophilite.

Mallarmé once wrote to Carondel: "Mon art est une impasse." He is right, but Valéry sits at the end of the cul-de-sac, as the final disciple of a sterile art. *He* will not leave any heirs. If the end of this blind corridor could be opened, there would be only *Le Néant, le gouffre* of Baudelaire.

BIBLIOGRAPHY

MALLARMÉ, STÉPHANE. *Œuvres complètes,* texte établi et annoté par Henri Mondor et G. Jean-Aubry. Bibliothèque de la Pléiade. Paris: Gallimard, 1945.
———*Poésies,* édition complète, contenant plusieurs poèmes inédits. Paris: NRF, 1913.
———"Ouverture ancienne d'Hérodiade," *Nouvelle Revue Française,* 1er novembre 1926. [In line 14, prints "Ou."]
———*Vers et prose. Morceaux choisis.* Paris: Perrin, 1893.
———*Divagations.* Paris: Fasquelle, 1897.
———*Propos sur la poésie,* recueillis et presentés par Henri Mondor. Paris: Plon, 1946.

AISH, DEBORAH A. K. *La Métaphore dans l'œuvre de Stéphane Mallarmé.* Paris: Droz, 1938.
———"La Rêve de Stéphane Mallarmé d'après sa correspondance," *PMLA,* Vol. LVI (1941), pp. 874–884.
AUSTIN, LLOYD J. "Mallarmé et le rêve du 'Livre,'" *Mercure de France,* 1er janvier 1953, pp. 81–108.
———"'Le principal pilier': Mallarmé, Victor Hugo et Richard Wagner," *Revue d'Histoire Littéraire de la France,* avril-juin 1951, pp. 154–180.
BEAUBOURG, MAURICE. "La Toussaint," *Revue Blanche,* Vol. XX (1899), pp. 331–339.
BEAUSIRE, PIERRE. *Essai sur la poésie et la poétique de Mallarmé.* Lausanne: Roth, 1942.
BONNIOT, EDMOND. "La Genèse poétique de Mallarmé d'après ses corrections," *Revue de France,* 15 avril 1929, pp. 631–644.

BOWRA, C. M. *The Heritage of Symbolism*. London: Macmillan, 1943.

CARRÈRE, JEAN. *Les Mauvais Maîtres*. Paris: Plon-Nourrit, 1922.

CHASSÉ, CHARLES. *Les Clés de Mallarmé*. Paris: Aubier, 1954.

———"Essai d'une interprétation objective du 'Tombeau d'Edgar Poe,' ou Mallarmé traduit par Mallarmé lui-même," *Revue de Littérature Comparée,* janvier-mars 1949, pp. 97-109.

———"Existe-t-il une clé de Mallarmé?" *Revue d'Histoire Littéraire de la France,* juillet-septembre 1952, pp. 352–366.

———*Lueurs sur Mallarmé*. Paris: NRF, 1947.

CHISHOLM, A. R. *An Approach to M. Valéry's Jeune Parque*. Melbourne Univ. Press, 1938.

———*The Art of Arthur Rimbaud*. Melbourne Univ. Press, 1930.

———*Towards Hérodiade: A Literary Genealogy*. Melbourne Univ. Press, 1934.

DAVIES, GARDNER. *Les "Tombeaux" de Mallarmé*. Paris: Corti, 1950.

DELFEL, GUY. *L'Esthétique de Stéphane Mallarmé*. Paris: Flammarion, 1951.

DUJARDIN, EDOUARD. *De Stéphane Mallarmé au prophète Ezéchiel*. Paris: Mercure de France, 1919.

———*Mallarmé, par un des siens*. Paris: Messein, 1936.

ELLIS, ARTHUR. *Stéphane Mallarmé in English Verse*. London: Cape, 1927.

FABUREAU, HUBERT. "Aspects de Mallarmé," *Nouvelle Revue Critique,* 17e année (1933), pp. 481-489.

———*Stéphane Mallarmé. Son œuvre*. Paris: Nouvelle Revue Critique, 1933.

FAURE, GABRIEL. *Mallarmé à Tournon*. Paris: Horizons de France, 1946.

Fowlie, Wallace. *Mallarmé.* Univ. of Chicago Press, 1953.

Fry, Roger, trans. *Stéphane Mallarmé: Poems,* with commentaries by Charles Mauron. New York: Oxford Univ. Press, 1937.

Gengoux, Jacques. *Le Symbolisme de Mallarmé.* Paris: Nizet, 1950.

George, Stefan. *Zeitgenössische Dichter.* Berlin: Georg Bondi, 1905.

Ghil, René. *Les Dates et les Œuvres. Symbolisme et poésie scientifique.* Paris: Crès, 1923.

Gourmont, Remy de. *Le Livre des masques.* Paris: Mercure de France, 1896.

——*Promenades littéraires,* II and IV. 4th ed., Paris: Mercure de France, 1913.

Kahn, Gustave. *Les Origines du symbolisme.* Paris: Messein, 1936.

——*Silhouettes littéraires.* Paris: Editions Montaigne, 1925.
——*Symbolistes et Décadents.* Paris: Vanier, 1902.

Lowell, Amy. *Six French Poets.* New York: Macmillan, 1916.

Mauclair, Camille. *L'Art en silence. L'Esthétique de Stéphane Mallarmé.* Paris: Ollendorff, 1901.

——*Mallarmé chez lui.* Paris: Grasset, 1935.
——*Princes de l'esprit.* Paris: Ollendorff, 1920.
——*Stéphane Mallarmé.* Paris: Société Nouvelle, 1894.

Mauron, Charles. *Mallarmé l'obscur.* Paris: Denoël, 1941.

Michaud, Guy. *Mallarmé. L'Homme et l'œuvre.* Paris: Hatier-Boivin, 1953.

Mondor, Henri. *Histoire d'un Faune.* Paris: Gallimard, 1948.

——*Mallarmé plus intime.* Paris: Gallimard, 1944.
——*Vie de Mallarmé.* Paris: Gallimard, 1941.

Moore, George. *Avowals.* New York: Boni & Liveright, 1919.

——*Confessions of a Young Man.* London: Laurie, 1904.

NOBILING, FRANZ. "Die Hérodiade Mallarmés," *Zeitschrift für französische Sprache und Litteratur,* Band LIII, Hefte 4, 5, 6 (1930), pp. 218–242.

———"Mallarmés Prose pour Des Esseintes," *ibid.,* Band LI, Hefte 7, 8 (1928), pp. 419–436.

———"Mallarméübersetzungen," *Idealistische Philologie,* Band III (1927), pp. 321–331.

NORDAU, MAX. *Zeitgenössische Französen.* Berlin: Hofmann, 1901.

NOULET, Mme E. *L'Œuvre poétique de Stéphane Mallarmé.* Paris: Droz, 1940.

Nouvelle Revue Française. Hommage à Stéphane Mallarmé, 1er novembre 1926.

Nouvelles Littéraires. Hommage à Stéphane Mallarmé, 13 octobre 1923.

ORLIAC, ANTOINE. *Mallarmé tel qu'en lui-même.* Paris: Mercure de France, 1948.

RAUHUT, FRANZ. *Das Romantische und Musikalische in der Lyrik Stéphane Mallarmés. (Die neueren Sprachen,* Beiheft nr. 11.) Marburg: Elwert, 1926.

RAYMOND, MARCEL. *De Baudelaire au surréalisme.* Paris: Correâ, 1933.

RAYNAUD, ERNEST. *La Mêlée symboliste.* Paris: Renaissance du Livre, 1920.

RÉGNIER, HENRI DE. *Nos rencontres.* Paris: Mercure de France, 1931.

———*Proses datées.* Paris: Mercure de France, 1925.

REIDEMEISTER, KURT. *Stéphane Mallarmé. Dichtungen.* Krefeld: Scherpe-Verlag, 1948.

RILKE, RAINER MARIA. *Gesammelte Werke,* Band VI. Leipzig: Insel-Verlag, 1927.

ROULET, CLAUDE. *Eléments de poétique mallarméenne.* Neuchâtel: Editions du Griffon, 1947.

ROYÈRE, JEAN. *Mallarmé.* Paris: Messein, 1931.

SCHERER, JACQUES. *L'Expression littéraire dans l'œuvre de Mallarmé.* Paris: Droz, 1947.

SOULA, CAMILLE. *Gloses sur Mallarmé*. Paris: Diderot, 1946.

————*La Poésie et la pensée de Stéphane Mallarmé: Essai sur l'hermétisme mallarméen*, 1926; *Le Symbole de la chevelure*, 1926; *Notes sur le Toast funèbre*, 1929. Paris: Champion.

SYMONS, ARTHUR. *The Symbolist Movement in Literature*. London: Heinemann, 1899.

THIBAUDET, ALBERT. *La Poésie de Stéphane Mallarmé*. 3d ed., Paris: NRF, 1926.

TURQUET-MILNES, G. "Stéphane Mallarmé: A Critical Study," Introduction to Arthur Ellis's *Stéphane Mallarmé in English Verse*, q.v. above.

USINGER, FRITZ. *Stéphane Mallarmé. Gedichte*. Jena: Karl Rauch Verlag, 1947.

VALÉRY, PAUL. *Ecrits divers sur Stéphane Mallarmé*. Paris: NRF, 1950.

————*Variété* II. Paris: Gallimard, 1930.

VERLAINE, PAUL. *Les Poètes maudits*. Paris: Vanier, 1884.

WAIS, KURT. *Mallarmé*. Munich: C. H. Beck'sche Verlagsbuchhandlung, 1938; 2d ed., 1952. All my references are to the 1938 edition.

WILSON, EDMUND. *Axel's Castle*. New York: Scribner's, 1931.

WOOLLEY, GRANGE. *Stéphane Mallarmé*. Madison, N.J.: Drew University, 1942.

WYZEWA, TÉODOR DE. "M. Mallarmé. Notes," *La Vogue*, nº 11, 5 au 12 juillet 1886, pp. 361–375; nº 12, 12 au 19 juillet 1886, pp. 414–424.

————*Nos maîtres*. Paris: Perrin, 1895.

C. F. MacINTYRE has suggested that he is an indefatigable translator partly because of the international interests of his family: his mother was a student of Latin and Greek, and his father was deeply interested in France and Egypt. Much of MacIntyre's life has been spent abroad, in various parts of Europe and in Mexico. German is his second language, and he took his Ph.D. at the University of Marburg. (There he began his translations of *Faust*, Part I, which first won him notice as a translator.) He now lives in Paris and devotes himself to translating, in support of which he has received Guggenheim and Fulbright grants.

MacIntyre is also known for his original poems, of which several volumes have been published: *Cafés and Cathedrals, The Black Bull,* and *Poems.*